TO ADRIANNE

er FRANCESCO

Sincerely.

Alain Ducasse   New York

le 5

XII

302

londres tokyo paris île maurice

alain

spa

food

ducasse
on
& wine

photography hartmut kiefer
artistic direction bernard père

conran
OCTOPUS

to Gwenaëlle

First published by Editions Noesis in 2001
30 Rue de Charonne, Paris

This edition published in 2002 by
Conran Octopus Limited
A part of Octopus Publishing Group
2–4 Heron Quays
London E14 4JP

www.conran-octopus.co.uk

ISBN 1 84091 261 8

Publishing Director: Lorraine Dickey
Senior Editor: Katey Day
Editor: Hilaire Walden

Creative Director: Leslie Harrington
Creative Manager: Lucy Gowans
Designer: Jeremy Tilston

Production Manager: Adam Smith

British Library Cataloguing-in-Publication Data
A catalogue record for this book is available from the British
Library

Printed and bound in China

Please note: Eggs should be medium unless otherwise stated.
Fresh herbs should be used unless otherwise stated. Pepper
should be freshly ground black pepper unless otherwise stated.

spoon user's guide

alain ducasse

I have set out to select recipes that will find favour with today's generation of up-to-the-minute gourmands, appeal to different cultures and tastes, and be in tune with present trends. I remember all the dinners with Gwenaëlle as my companion. She wanted vegetables, but no artichokes, or carrots or potatoes; a vinaigrette without oil or vinegar but with lemon juice… It wasn't difficult to reconcile the English way of doing things with the preferences of France and elsewhere. What had started out as a considerable problem became an unalloyed pleasure, and working out the menus for Spoon was a real treat.

It goes without saying that the agreeable hotchpotch of influences, which has subtly changed the management of our houses, our music and the way we dress, had already made its way into our kitchens almost before we were aware of it. For several generations, different regions and countries have interacted with each other. But, a word of caution! Please don't put words into my mouth: I don't believe that there has been a loss of identity but, rather, that there is a greater awareness of each other. One country's coarsely ground pepper is another's sprinkling of lemon juice; freedom is everything.

This involves a spirit of exploration, analysis and iconoclasm. Do you feel like adding tomato to this fish, or to that chicken? And why not? I have always believed that there is an inner voice which prompts you to take, and eat, a certain food in preference to any other. This is what appeals to me about Spoon's cooking.

Anyway, that is how this book was designed. You will see that there are no one-way streets, that you are not trapped on a 'motorway' of taste. It's a case of 'as you like it'. If you want to take a side turning, reverse, start again, no one will stop you. But, when it comes to stopping short – no way! If you choose to have mustard velouté sauce instead of a choice of lemon sauces, that's no problem. Or if you prefer your potatoes stir-fried in a wok rather than cooked à la Maxim: go ahead. In this sense, the cooking of Spoon is instinctive: chew, munch, eat, drink. These 'deconstructed' dishes have all the adaptability of basic cooking. What I like about the ethos of Spoon is that it combines the simplest, most fundamental gesture – dipping a spoon into an earthenware bowl – with modern sophistication.

What Spoon has taught me is that life is a chameleon: it takes on the colours of our desires. In Mauritius, Tokyo, Paris and London where the Spoon restaurants have opened, their cooking immediately found its mark, hitting the right spot and, after some fine-tuning, was thoroughly at home.

Something else that I learned from Spoon was that cooking opens up wide horizons for us. The cobwebs are swept out of our minds. The regimented discipline that tells us to do such-and-such, open this, shut that, and similar cast-iron rules, is banished: classical training underpins tremendous freedom. To each their own. Spoon meant that I could opt to create a crayfish club sandwich, a Malabar ice; achieve a fresh take on existing recipes and discover new ones.

With this book I feel as if my cooking has taken on a new, free, cheeky and slightly provocative personality, which is unlike that of my forebears, but it is what today's food lovers want.

c   o   n   t

1

appetizers

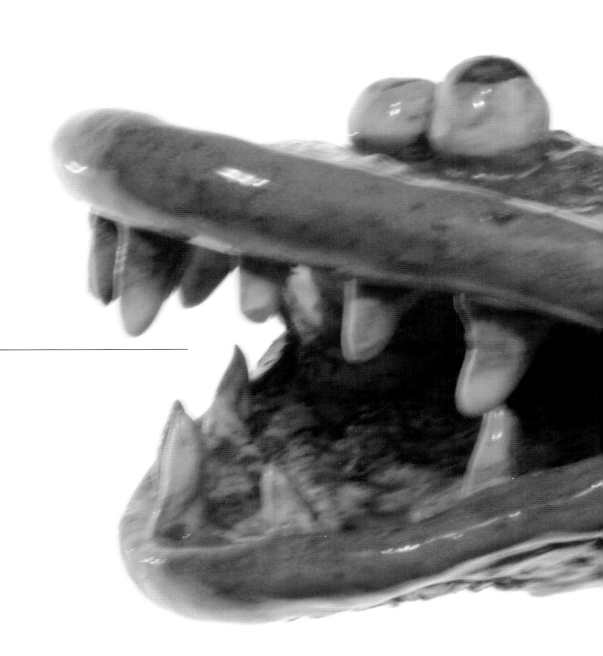

serves 4: 250 g dried, salt cod   500 ml milk   1 sprig of thyme   2 tbsp olive oil
3 cloves garlic, crushed   50 g parsley, finely chopped   pepper   oil for deep-frying
fritter batter: 200 g plain flour   pinch of chilli powder   pinch of instant dried yeast
salt   100 ml milk   2 egg whites, whisked   **chilli tomato sauce:**
4 large, fat spring onions, white part only, finely chopped   200 ml tomato juice
dash of Tabasco sauce   dash of garlic chilli sauce   1/2 tsp fresh ginger, finely grated

creole cod fritters
chilli tomato sauce

1 Soak the cod in water for 24 hours, changing the water four times. Drain the cod and put in a saucepan with the milk and thyme and 500 ml water. Bring to boiling point and poach for 10 minutes. Drain off the liquid and crush the cod to a purée, gradually adding the olive oil, garlic and parsley. Season with pepper and set aside. **2** To make the fritter batter, mix the flour with the chilli pepper, yeast and a pinch of salt, then slowly add the milk to make a thick batter. Leave for 1 hour, then add to the cod purée, a little at a time, working it in until the mixture is smooth. Fold in the egg whites. **3** Half-fill a large, heavy saucepan with oil and heat to 180ºC. Shape the fish mixture into small balls and add to the hot oil in batches. When the balls start to brown, remove with a slotted spoon and drain on kitchen paper. Keep warm while frying the remaining balls. **4** To make the sauce, combine all the ingredients. **5** Serve the cod fritters very hot, accompanied by the sauce.

1 Use a mandolin to slice all the vegetables except the broccoli and cauliflower, then put in a very large bowl of iced water. **2** Steam the broccoli florets until tender, then plunge into iced water and drain again. Purée with 100 ml white stock. Add a good dash of olive oil and season with salt and pepper. Spoon into a small serving bowl and set aside. **3** Repeat with the cauliflower. **4** Sprinkle the bread slices with the chosen spice. Place in a heated oven until crisp. **5** Drain the sliced vegetables very well and arrange on a large platter. Serve with two cold purées as sauces, and the spiced toast.

raw vegetable chips

serves 4: 1 large fennel bulb   1 head of celery   4 very fresh carrots
12 green asparagus spears   1 bunch of baby turnips   1 black radish   300 g mooli
1/2 bunch round, red radishes   1 large broccoli   200 ml white stock (page 126)   olive oil
salt   pepper   1 small cauliflower, divided into florets   French stick, thinly sliced
curry, paprika or chilli, for sprinkling

serves 8: 2 crabs or 400 g crab meat   100 ml sauce américaine (page 127)
30 g butter, diced   salt   pepper   oil, for deep-frying
white sauce: 75 g butter   75 g plain flour   1 litre whole milk
egg and breadcrumb coating: 50 g potato flour   2 egg yolks   1/2 tsp olive oil
pinch of sugar   pinch of salt   300 g fine dry breadcrumbs

crab cakes

appetizers

1 Cook the crabs in barely simmering water for 15 minutes. Extract all the flesh and flake with a fork. **2** Heat the sauce américaine, uncovered, to reduce and thicken it. **3** Make the white sauce (see method page 88) and stir in the sauce américaine and crab meat and then gradually add the butter. Season with salt and pepper. **4** Chill until firm, then shape into 1 cm balls. **5** To coat the fish balls, roll them in the potato flour. Mix the egg yolks, oil, sugar and salt. Dip the balls in this and then coat in breadcrumbs. **6** Half-fill a large, heavy pan with oil and heat to 180ºC. Lower in the fish balls in batches. Fry for 2 minutes, then transfer to kitchen paper to drain. Serve very hot.

11

1 Use a melon-baller to scoop out balls from the carrots and courgettes. **2** Sweat the vegetables (adding them in the order given below) with the coriander; do not allow to brown. **3** Add the wine and vinegar to the pan; stir with a wooden spoon, then add the thyme, bay leaf and white stock. **4** Cook very gently for a few minutes and then leave to cool. Season with salt and pepper. **5** Add the freshly chopped coriander leaves. **6** Discard the muslin bag of coriander seeds, then chill the vegetables until required.

crudités à la greque

appetizers

serves 4: 3 very fresh large carrots   2 courgettes   1/2 cauliflower, divided into small florets
18 baby onions   12 baby fennel bulbs   12 large spring onions   300 g button mushrooms
2 tbsp coriander seeds tied in a muslin bag   200 ml dry white wine
100 ml white wine vinegar   sprig of thyme   bay leaf   600 ml white stock (page 126)
salt and pepper   1/2 bunch of coriander

serves 4: 3 cucumbers   handful of mint, chopped   1/2 handful of coriander, chopped
2–2 1/2 tbsp sherry vinegar   3 dashes of Tabasco sauce
4 tomatoes, skinned, all seeds and stalk removed, cut into 5 mm dice
100 g soft goats' cheese

iced cucumber soup

1 Peel off alternating lengthwise strips from the cucumbers (see picture below). **2** Discard the seeds from half a cucumber, and cut into 5 mm dice; set aside. Purée the other 2 1/2 cucumbers, and chill. **3** Add the mint and coriander leaves, and sherry vinegar and Tabasco to taste. Like gazpacho, this soup should be acidulated and strongly-flavoured. **4** Mix the diced cucumber with the tomatoes and place one quarter of this in each serving bowl. Pour in the soup and put a rounded spoonful of goats' milk cheese on top.

serves 4: 100 g very fresh, raw bluefin tuna   50 g fresh seaweed (nori or wakame) generous pinch of salt   generous pinch of pepper
mayonnaise: 2 egg yolks   1/2 tsp Savora mustard   300 ml peanut oil   juice of 1 lime salt   pepper   1/2 tsp wasabi   Tabasco sauce

tuna tartare

1 Cut the tuna into small cubes and finely shred the seaweed. **2** To make the mayonnaise, mix the egg yolks with the mustard then gradually beat in the oil. Add the lime juice and seasoning, then some wasabi and Tabasco to taste. **3** Mix the mayonnaise with the tuna and seaweed and season with salt and pepper. **4** Serve immediately.

serves 4: 2 fennel bulbs, hearts only, chopped   2 courgettes   1 stick of celery
2 green apples   200 g Saint-Moret soft cheese, or drained fromage frais
small bunch of chives   2–3 sprigs of mint   2–3 sprigs of coriander
1/2 tsp chilli powder   salt   pepper   juice of 2 limes   dash of Tabasco sauce
leaves of 1/2 Cos lettuce or French bread croutons, to serve

vegetable tartare

appetizers

1 Chop the vegetables and apples separately. **2** Put in a salad bowl and gently fold in the soft cheese. **3** Use scissors to snip the chives, mint and coriander leaves over the vegetables and sprinkle with chilli powder, salt and pepper. **4** Add the lime juice, and Tabasco sauce to taste; the salad should be quite spicy. **5** Serve with Cos leaves, or croutons.

15

1 In a deep frying pan or saucepan, bring the rice wine vinegar to the boil with the pickled ginger, chillies and sugar. **2** Add the spring onions, garlic and diced pumpkin. Cook for 10 minutes, then add the raisins and leave until cold. **3** Add the strips of pumpkin, the fresh ginger, basil and the almonds or pumpkin seeds.

appetizers

pumpkin chutney

serves 4: 200 ml rice wine vinegar   28 g Japanese pickled ginger, finely chopped   2 bird's eye chillies   75 g brown cane sugar   25 g large spring onions, white part only, sliced into thin rings   2 cloves garlic, finely chopped   300 g pumpkin, cut into 5 mm cubes   50 g raisins   150 g pumpkin, cut into very thin strips   25 g finely chopped fresh ginger   2 basil leaves, finely chopped   60 g toasted almonds or pumpkin seeds

2

starters

salads

serves 4: court bouillon (page 126)   4 live lobsters weighing 450–500 g each
wines: South Africa: white Walker Bay 1998 Chardonnay Mission Vale Bouchard
France: Champagne Noble Cuvée 1988 Lanson

salads

lobster salad

1 Bring the court bouillon to the boil in a large saucepan and plunge in the live lobsters. Boil for 8 minutes then remove from the liquid and leave to cool. **2** Slice the cooled lobsters lengthwise in half and remove the white tail meat in 8 whole pieces. Wrap each matching pair in a clean, damp cloth. Reserve the coral. **3** Remove claw meat from the shell as neatly as possible and then assemble each lobster's flesh on an individual plate. **4** Serve with your preferred sauce and a seasonal vegetable.

22

ancholive 108

green beans
fresh almonds

▽ **sauce**   ▲ **accompaniment**

coral mustard

coral from 4 hen (female) lobsters
250 ml olive oil
1 1/2 tsp Meaux mustard
1 tsp Dijon mustard
2 tbsp sherry vinegar
salt
pepper
1 tbsp finely chopped tarragon
1/2 tsp finely chopped chervil

Gently cook the coral in a little of the oil in a heavy pan until it turns a bright orange-red. Transfer to a bowl and leave to cool. Then mix with the mustards, vinegar and season lightly. Gradually whisk in the remaining oil, as for vinaigrette. Add the tarragon and chervil. Only female, or 'hen', lobsters have coral, or eggs; ask the fishmonger to select them for you.

serves 4: 100 g sprouting lucerne   100 g sprouting wheat
100 g sprouting lentils or mung beans   100 g sprouting coriander seeds
100 g mustard and cress   olive oil   juice of 2 lemons   salt   pepper
wines: Australia: white Margaret River 1998 Verdelho Abbey Vale
France: Corsica white Patrimonio 1998 Arena

salads

sprouting salad

1 Mix all the sprouting seeds and vegetables, the sprouting coriander seeds and the mustard and cress. **2** Whisk together a good dash of oil and the lemon juice and toss with the salad. **3** Season with salt and pepper. **4** Serve with blue cheese sauce, aubergine pickle and prawns.

24

▲ aubergine pickle 102   ▲ prawns

▼ **sauce**   ▲ **accompaniment**

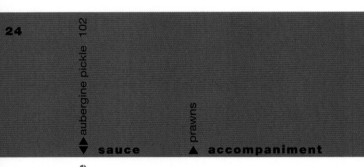

blue cheese sauce

2 tbsp Savora mustard
2 egg yolks
250 ml peanut oil
50 g Stilton or Bleu d'Auvergne, beaten to soften
juice of 1/2 lemon
seasoning (optional)
diced Stilton, for garnish

Work the mustard into the yolks in a bowl and gradually beat in the oil. When the sauce starts to thicken, gradually add the cheese. Add enough lemon juice to thin the sauce slightly, and season if necessary. Garnish with diced Stilton.

serves 4: 8 white, or white and green chicory heads
2 Treviso-type pinkish-red chicory heads   1 curly endive or frisé heart
wines: United States: white Santa Barbara Country 1997 Pinot blanc Au Bon Climat
France: Alsace blanc Sylvaner Les Vieilles Vignes 1998 Ostertag

salads **endives**

1 Cut off the bases of the chicory heads, divide into leaves and reserve the outer leaves to garnish the salad. Divide the curly endive heart into leaves. **2** Slice the chicory hearts into thin strips. **3** Add the accompaniment of your choice and serve with the mustard dressing separately.

26

▼ walnut relish 104

▼ **sauce**

▲ crisp bacon

▲ **accompaniment**

mustard dressing

2 tbsp traditional, coarse-grain mustard
2 tbsp Dijon mustard
1 tbsp wine vinegar
250 ml grapeseed oil
salt
pepper

Use a balloon whisk to blend the two mustards, then beat in the vinegar followed by the oil, adding a little at a time. Season with salt and pepper.

serves 4: Approximately 600g in total of assorted wild and water-grown salads, such as: watercress, purslane, chickweed, mustard and cress, soya bean sprouts
Wines: United States: white Santa Barbara County 1996 Aligoté Au Bon Climat
France: Bordeaux blanc Côtes-de-Francs 1998 Château Les Charmes Godard

salads **salade d'o'**

1 Mix the chosen salad greens together, then add the dressing and serve.

28

oyster and lemon 108

soft-boiled egg

▲ **dressing**   ▲ **accompaniment**

29

1 Arrange the flowers with the salad greens and herbs in a salad bowl.
2 Add the ancholive and serve.

salads

salad of flowers
and bitter salad herbs

serves 4: edible flowers in season such as garlic, chives, basil, nasturtiums, pansies
bitter herbs and salad greens: 150 g purslane   150 g rocket   150 g wild rocket (riquette)
small bunch of sorrel   4–5 sprigs of chervil   small bunch of chives, chopped
2 sprigs of tarragon   2 sprigs of marjoram
wines: Argentina: white   Mendoza 1999   Torrontes   Santa Julia
France: Provence   white   Côtes-de-Provence   1997   Château Sainte-Marguerite   Fayard

ancholive 108

▲ **accompaniment**

serves 4: 1 fennel bulb   1 celery heart   12 green asparagus spears   6 large, very fresh carrots
1 cucumber   1 bunch of red radishes   1 black radish   8 spring onions
4 vine tomatoes, skinned, quartered, deseeded and cut into 'petals'   100 g rocket
wines: New Zealand: white Hawkes Bay 1999 Sauvignon Trinity Hill
France: Côtes-du-Rhône white 1997 Coudoulet de Beaucastel Perrin

spoon's crudités

1 Using a mandolin, thinly slice the vegetables, except the tomatoes and rocket. Soak in a bowl of iced water for about 15 minutes. **2** Drain the vegetables very well and arrange on salad plates, adding the tomato 'petals' and the rocket leaves. **3** Serve with your choice of dressing.

spicy tomato coulis 68   salted anchovies
▲ **dressing** ▲ **accompaniment**

serves 4: 4 Cos lettuce hearts
wines: **Australia:** white Eden Valley 1997 Riesling Henschke-Julius
France: Loire Valley white 1995 Vouvray Le Mont Domaine Huet

salads

cos salad

1 Separate the leaves of the lettuce hearts and place in a salad bowl. **2** Add the dressing and accompaniment of your choice

34

◄ horseradish 109

prawns
croutons

▼ **dressing**   ▲ **accompaniment**

caesar dressing

2 egg yolks
2 hard-boiled eggs, chopped
6 anchovy fillets (rinsed if salted), chopped
2 cloves garlic, crushed
50 g freshly grated Parmesan cheese
juice of 1 lemon
200 ml grapeseed oil
dash of Worcestershire sauce
dash of Tabasco sauce
1 tbsp sherry vinegar

Place the egg yolks in a bowl and mix in the hard-boiled eggs, anchovies, garlic, Parmesan and lemon juice. Gradually mix in the oil, as when making mayonnaise. Flavour generously with Worcestershire sauce and Tabasco sauce and add sherry vinegar to taste.

soups

soups

green soup of herbs, salad greens, cucumber and crème fraîche

38

1 Bring a large saucepan of salted water to the boil, then plunge in the lettuces, watercress and parsley. Remove immediately. **2** Plunge into iced water to refresh. Drain, then purée with the white stock. Strain through a conical sieve and season to taste. **3** Peel off alternate lengthwise strips of the cucumber's skin (see picture on page 12); scoop out all the seeds from the centre and cut the flesh into small cubes. **4** For the herbs and salad greens, sprinkle the basil, coriander and mint leaves with a little sea salt, and mix with the rocket and Cos leaves. **5** Place a rounded tablespoonful of crème fraîche in each soup bowl. Divide the cucumber cubes among the bowls and add a small heap of mixed bitter salad. **6** Ladle in the green soup, either cold (in summer) or hot (in winter); do not allow it to boil or it will lose its fresh green colour.

1 sprig of basil   1 sprig of coriander   1 sprig of mint   sea salt   50 g rocket   50 g Cos lettuce leaves
wines : United States: white California 1996 Aligoté Au Bon Climat
France : Burgundy white 1998 Chablis J.-P. Droin

serves 4: 30 frogs' legs 2 tablespoons olive oil 50 g butter, plus 2–3 tbsp for cooking 3 shallots, finely sliced 3 cloves garlic 1/2 stick of celery 200 ml dry white wine 650 ml double cream 1/2 bunch of watercress 1/2 bunch of flat leaf parsley
wines: United States: white Santa Barbara County 1997 Pinot gris Domaine Santa Barbara
France: Burgundy white Côte Chalonnaise 1998 Givry Premier Cru Clos de la Servoisine Joblot

frogs' legs soup

1 Bone the frogs' legs. Keep the trimmings to make the stock. **2** Heat the olive oil and less than half the butter in a saucepan. **3** Fry the frogs' legs trimmings without allowing them to brown. **4** Add the shallots, garlic and celery, reserving 4 small sprigs for garnishing. Cover and cook gently until softened. **5** Pour in the white wine, scraping any deposits loose. Boil, uncovered until reduced by half. Add 500 ml cream and simmer gently for 30 minutes, uncovered. **6** Pass through a vegetable mill then blend in the remaining butter in a food processor or with a hand-held mixer. Return to the saucepan and reheat gently. **7** Reserve 4 sprigs each of the watercress and parsley. Add the remaining parsley and watercress to a large pan of boiling salted water. Remove immediately, drain and refresh straight away in iced water. Purée and set aside. **8** Heat 2–3 tablespoons butter until golden brown then sauté the frogs' legs. Remove and keep hot. **9** Divide the frogs' legs among 4 warm wide, deep plates and add the reserved sprigs of watercress, parsley and celery. **10** Whisk the remaining cream until stiff. Put a tablespoonful in each bowl and season. **11** Blend the green purée into the soup with a hand-held mixer. Pour into bowls and serve at once.

41

serves 4: minestrone garnish: 1 onion   1 small turnip   1 carrot   50 g fresh haricot beans   25 g butter   2 cloves garlic, bruised   1 courgette   10 basil leaves   5 sticks of celery   3 crabs   court bouillon (page 126)   2 blanched nori leaves   2 celery leaves   2 tbsp pesto
aromatic broth: 1 onion   1 small turnip   1 carrot   1 courgette   25 g butter   3 leaves of fresh nori seaweed   100 ml dry white wine   1 litre white stock (page 126)   500 ml cream   salt   pepper
wines: New Zealand: white Hawkes Bay 1999 Sauvignon Cape Crest Te Mata
France: Loire Valley white 1996 Pouilly fumé Cuvée Majorum Michel Redde & fils

soups

minestrone of crab
and nori

1 To make the minestrone mixture, finely chop all the vegetables. Sweat the onion, turnip, carrot and haricot beans in a little butter for 10 minutes in a covered saucepan. Add 1 garlic clove, the courgette, basil, celery and cook for 5 minutes longer. Season and stir in the remaining garlic. Leave to cool. **2** Remove the crabs' claws and legs and place these and the bodies in the court bouillon and boil gently for 8 minutes. **3** To make the aromatic broth, finely chop the vegetables and sweat them in a little butter in a covered heavy pan, without browning. **4** Remove all the meat from the crabs' bodies (and legs if wished) and add to the heavy pan with the 3 fresh nori leaves. Pour in the wine, loosening any deposits with a wooden spoon; cook, uncovered, until reduced by half and then add enough stock to come half-way up the ingredients. Simmer for 20 minutes. **5** Add the cream and cook for a further 10 minutes. Purée until smooth then strain through a conical sieve into a saucepan. **6** Season with salt and pepper and keep hot. Remove the flesh from the crabs' claws and add to the minestrone mixture (discard the garlic cloves). Add the coarsely chopped blanched nori leaves, the chopped celery leaves and half the pesto. **7** Spread about 1/2 teaspoon of the remaining pesto on each of 4 small plates. Use a slotted spoon to transfer the vegetable mixture to the plates. **8** Add the claw meat and sprinkle with a little coarse salt. Serve the soup in heated soup bowls.

42

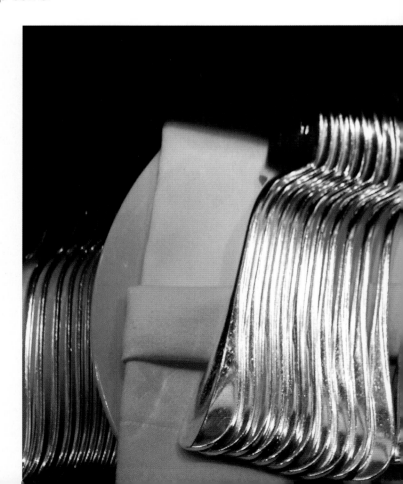

serves 4: 2 tbsp olive oil   2 onions   500 g slice of pumpkin   salt   pepper
250 ml crème fraîche   about 500 ml white stock (page 126)   stiffly whipped cream to serve
wines: New Zealand: white Marlborough 1999 Sauvignon Cloudy Bay
France: Burgundy white Côte chalonnaise 1997 Mercurey-Les-Croichots B. Lorenzon

pumpkin soup
with pumpkin garnish

soups

1 Heat the olive oil in a saucepan. Add the finely sliced onions, cover and leave to cook gently. **2** Use a serrated knife to peel the pumpkin, then scrape off the seeds and threads. **3** Set aside a fairly thick slice. Cut the rest of the flesh into small pieces and add to the onions. Season, cover and cook for a further 10 minutes. **4** Add the crème fraîche to the saucepan, followed by enough stock to cover the vegetables completely. Leave to boil gently for 20 minutes, stirring frequently. **5** Cut the reserved slice of pumpkin into 5 mm dice and fry in olive oil until just tender. Season with salt and pepper and transfer to a sieve to drain off excess oil. **6** Purée the soup in batches, and pour each batch through a conical sieve into the top of a double boiler, if possible, to keep hot. Adjust the seasoning. **7** Spoon the diced pumpkin garnish into 4 heated soup plates, add 1 tablespoon stiffly whipped cream and pour in the hot soup.

43

serves 4: 500 g raw brown shrimps   1/3 lemon grass bulb   1 thin slice of galangal
1 thin slice of fresh ginger   1 bird's eye chilli   1 tomato   1 litre white stock (page 126)
pepper   2 egg whites   **accompaniment:** 1 garlic clove   2 shallots   5–6 sprigs of parsley
1 fennel bulb   1 carrot   20 g mignonette pepper   parsley   200 ml dry white wine
seafood: 100 g cockles   8 carpet shell clams   50 g dog cockles   100 g squid
4 tiger prawn tails   20 g mignonette pepper   50 g fresh wakame   1 crab
4 raw scallops, thinly sliced   pinch of finely grated fresh ginger
wines: United States: white   Santa Barbara County   1998   Viognier   Andrew Murray Vineyards
France: Alsace: white   1996   Riesling   Cuvée Frédéric Emile F.E.Trimbach

soups

'youm-koumg' soup

1 Put the brown shrimps, lemon grass, galangal, ginger, coarsely-chopped chilli and tomato, and the stock in a large saucepan. Season with pepper. **2** Bring to the boil, stirring. Add the egg whites and stir with a balloon whisk to clarify the broth. Reduce the heat to as low as possible so the liquid barely bubbles and cook for 20 minutes. **3** Line a sieve with clean, damp muslin and place over the top of a large double boiler, or heatproof bowl placed over a saucepan. Ladle the broth very carefully into the sieve, to avoid releasing particles trapped in the egg white. Season the strained broth, if necessary. The broth should be very clear, aromatic and full-bodied. **4** Divide the vegetable accompaniment into 5 equal parts.

44

5 Cook the cockles, carpet shell clams, dog cockles, squid and prawns separately, each with a sixth of the vegetable accompaniments, 40 ml wine and a grinding of pepper. Immediately the shellfish open transfer to a platter and leave to cool. **6** Blanch the wakame for a few seconds, then refresh in iced water to fix its lovely colour. Drain and finely shred. **7** Bring a large saucepan of water to the boil, add the remaining portion of vegetable accompaniment and the crab; cook for 8 minutes. Leave to cool before removing all the flesh from the crab. **8** Place some wakame in the bottom of each soup bowl, add a portion of seafood, prawns, crab meat and the thinly-sliced scallops. Pour over the very hot broth and add the finely grated ginger. **9** This soup can be served hot, or cold (see jellied 'youm-koumg' page 49).

serves 8: cream of sweetcorn soup: 2 onions   4 leeks, green parts only   2 sticks of celery   6 tbsp olive oil   300 g crab meat   8 sweetcorn cobs   200 ml dry white wine   2 litres white stock (page 126)   salt   pepper   **spring rolls:** 8 sheets of brik pastry or egg roll wrappers about 18cm in diameter   1 egg white   1 litre vegetable oil for deep-frying

wines: Germany: white Moselle 1998 Riesling Spätlese Trocken Brauneberger-Juffer-Sonnenuhr Fritz Haag

France: Burgundy white Côtes-de-Beaune 1999 Ladoix-Les-Gréchons Capitain Gagnerot

soups

spring rolls with crab
and grapefruit filling
cream of sweetcorn soup

46

1 To make the soup, sweat the onion, leek and celery in a little oil until softened but not browned. **2** Add the crab meat and corn then pour in the wine, scraping off any deposits from the bottom of the pan with a wooden spoon. Boil, uncovered, until reduced by half. Add the stock. Simmer for 30 minutes. **3** Remove the corn and scrape off the kernels; set aside 200 g. Purée the remaining kernels with the contents of the saucepan, then strain through a conical sieve into a saucepan. Season and keep hot. **4** To make the filling, heat the oil in a wok. Add the carrots, cabbage, mushrooms, ginger and soy sauce and cook for 3 minutes. **5** Add the noodles and spring onion and cook for a further 2 minutes. **6** Transfer the ingredients to a bowl and stir in the crab meat, grapefruit zest and the reduced sauce américaine. Season with salt and pepper. **7** To make the spring rolls, working on a flat surface, fold the brik sheets in half. Spread one eighth of the filling near the folded edge of each sheet. Fold in the sides, then roll up to form a roll. Seal the edges with egg white. Repeat with the remaining filling and brik pastry, to make 8 spring rolls. **8** Half-fill a heavy-based pan with oil and heat to 150°C. Add the spring rolls and gradually increase the temperature to 180°C. Fry for 3–5 minutes until golden brown, turning to brown evenly. Transfer to kitchen paper to drain. Keep hot. **9** To serve, divide the reserved corn kernels among the serving bowls, place a spring roll on top and pour over the soup.

filling: 1 tbsp olive oil   100 g carrots, cut into thin strips
25 g white cabbage, finely shredded   50 g shiitake mushrooms, finely chopped
1/2 tsp finely chopped fresh ginger   1 tbsp soy sauce
40 g rice vermicelli, soaked in boiling water for 5 minutes, drained and snipped into short lengths
1 spring onion, sliced into thin rings   200g crab meat
shredded zest of 1 grapefruit, blanched once in boiling water and drained
2 tbsp sauce américaine (page 127), reduced to thicken

soup: serves 4: 500 g brown shrimps, unpeeled   1/2 lemon grass bulb
thin slice of fresh ginger   thin slice of galangal   1 bird's eye chilli, coarsely chopped
1 litre white stock (page 126)   1 tomato, chopped   pepper   2 egg whites   salt
3 gelatine leaves, soaked in cold water
wines: Lebanon: white Bekaa Valley 1990 Chardonnay-Sauvignon Château Musar
France: Bordeaux white Graves 1997 Château Chantgrive

48

seafood accompaniment: 4 quahogs (large clams)   8 carpet shell clams   50 g dog cockles
1 crab   200 ml dry white wine   50 g fresh wakame   250 ml coconut milk
4 raw scallops, white part only   8 tiger prawns or Mediterranean prawns
4 pinches finely grated fresh ginger

ginger confit: 1 large piece of fresh ginger, cut into thin strips   juice of 1 lime   80 g sugar
vegetable garnish: 1 garlic clove, coarsely chopped   2 shallots, coarsely chopped
5 sprigs flat leaf parsley, coarsely chopped   1 fennel bulb, coarsely chopped
1 carrot, coarsely chopped

jellied 'youm-koumg'

soups

49

1 To make the ginger confit, place the ginger in 100 ml cold water, bring to the boil, drain and leave to cool. Simmer the lime juice, 150 ml water and the sugar gently for 1 hour, then add the ginger. **2** Place the brown shrimps in a saucepan along with the lemon grass bulb, ginger, galangal, chilli, white stock and tomato. Season with pepper. **3** Process very briefly with a hand-held mixer and then bring slowly to a gentle boil. Add the egg whites and stir with a balloon whisk. Reduce the heat to very low and simmer very gently for 20 minutes. **4** Line a sieve with clean, damp muslin and place over the top of a double boiler, or a heatproof bowl over a saucepan. Ladle the broth into the sieve as gently as possible to avoid releasing matter from the egg white otherwise the broth will be cloudy. Adjust the seasoning of the broth and add the gelatine leaves. Leave to cool and set. **5** Rinse the shellfish very thoroughly to get rid of any sand. **6** Divide the vegetable garnish into 4 portions. Cook the quahogs, clams, dog cockles and crab separately with a portion of vegetables, 1/4 of the wine and a twist of the peppermill until the shells open. Transfer to a platter and leave to cool. Remove the flesh from the crab and cool. **7** Blanch the wakame for 2–3 seconds in boiling water, remove and place in iced water to fix its beautiful colour. Drain well and shred. **8** Boil the coconut milk, uncovered, until it is thick enough to coat the back of a wooden spoon, then leave to cool. **9** Divide the wakame among the serving bowls. Add a portion of crab meat, shellfish, finely sliced scallops and prawns. **10** Use a large spoon to stir the jelly until it has a wobbly but almost pouring consistency and spoon over the shellfish to cover it in a layer. Pour the coconut milk on top and add a pinch each of fresh ginger and ginger confit to each serving.

to**fu**

serves 4: 500 g button mushrooms, cut into thin strips   250 ml white stock (page 126)
200 ml UHT single cream   salt   pepper   2 eggs, beaten
100 g fresh shiitake mushrooms, cut into thin strips   100 g enoki mushrooms
olive oil, for cooking   juice of 1/2 lemon
wines: Austria: white Burgenland 1997 Golser Chardonnay George Lunzer
France: Jura white 1996 L'Étoile-en-Mont Genezet Domaine Voorhuis-Henquet

mushroom tofu

1 Cook the button mushrooms gently in a little butter in a saucepan
for 5 minutes, then add the white stock and cream and simmer
gently, covered, for 15 minutes. Season with salt and pepper.
Transfer the saucepan to a sink of iced water to cool the contents
rapidly. **2** Purée until smooth then strain through a conical sieve into
a bowl. Stir in the eggs until well blended. **3** Pour into small, deep
soup bowls and place in a roasting tin with enough hot water to
come half-way up the sides of the bowls. Put in the preheated oven
at 180°C/gas mark 4 for 25 minutes until lightly set. **4** Sauté the
shiitake and enoki mushrooms briefly in a little olive oil without
browning. Add the lemon juice. **5** Top the mushroom custards with
the green sauce (below) and place the mushrooms in the centre.

52

ENOKI IS A TALL, WHITE MUSHROOM THAT
CAN BE STIR-FRIED IN A WOK WITH A
LITTLE WHITE STOCK.

▼ **sauce**   ▲ **accompaniment**

green sauce

300 g spinach
1 bunch of flat leaf parsley leaves
6 garlic cloves, finely chopped
olive oil, for cooking
100 ml white stock (page 126)
salt
pepper

Cook the spinach, parsley and garlic
briefly in a little oil in a sauté pan. Add
the stock, simmer briefly and purée to
make a very smooth green sauce.
Season to taste.

serves 4: 600 g peeled pumpkin, preferably muscade   100 ml olive oil   5 sprigs of thyme
7 garlic cloves   salt   pepper   2 eggs   200 ml UHT single cream
1 slice of white bread, rubbed with garlic   8 slices of bacon   12 scallops, at room temperature
50 g roast hazelnuts, thinly sliced   2 tsp melted butter
wines: Italy: white Friuli-Venezia-Julia 1997 Savignon-Chardonnay-Ribolla Vintage Tunina
Sylvio Jermann   **France:** Burgundy white Côtes-de-Beaune 1994 Corton Charlemagne
Grand Cru Bouchard Père et Fils

tofu |pumpkin tofu with scallop topping

1 Cut the pumpkin into 3 mm cubes. Place a large sheet of foil on a baking sheet with enough overhanging to make the parcel (step 2). Spread 500 g of the pumpkin on the foil and brush liberally with oil. **2** Add 3 thyme sprigs, 5 garlic cloves, 1 teaspoon salt and 1/2 teaspoon pepper. Fold over the overlapping foil to make a loose parcel. Cook in a preheated oven at 170°C/gas mark 3 for 1 1/2 hours until the pumpkin flesh is easily squashed if pressed lightly with a finger. **3** Purée and leave to cool. **4** Add the eggs and cream and process until smooth.

54

beurre noisette ▲ **sauce**

5 Increase the oven temperature to 180°C/gas mark 4. Sauté the remaining pumpkin cubes in olive oil with the remaining thyme and garlic. **6** Divide these cubes among 4 soup bowls and pour on enough purée to come three-quarters of the way up the inside of the bowls. Stand them in a roasting tin, add sufficient hot water to come half-way up their sides and bake for 25 minutes or until lightly set. **7** Cut the bread and bacon into very thin strips. Fry the bread until lightly browned. Remove. Cook the bacon until fairly crisp, and remove. Leave the fat and juices in the pan. **8** Prepare the topping for each bowl separately, repeating this step and step 9. Thinly slice the white parts of 3 scallops, and overlap in a circle (see opposite) on top of a piece of greaseproof paper. Carefully place in the hot frying pan to cook for about 1–2 minutes. **9** Slide the scallops carefully on to the surface of a serving. Top with the bread strips, bacon and sliced hazelnuts and spoon over some of the melted butter. Repeat for the remaining servings.

steaming

serves 4: 20 nems: 1 Savoy cabbage   250 g waxy or salad potatoes   1 tbsp sea salt
2 garlic cloves, partially squashed   1 bay leaf   1 sprig of thyme   300 g pastrami, diced
300 g Granny Smith apples, diced   150 g gherkins, chopped   150 g lean veal, finely chopped
Savora sauce: 2 egg yolks   salt   pepper   2 tbsp Dijon mustard   50 g Savora mustard
200 ml grapeseed oil   juice of 1 lemon
wines: Germany: white Nahe 1997 Pinot gris Cuvée Victor Schlossgut Diel
France: Bordeaux white Graves 1987 Château Chantegrive

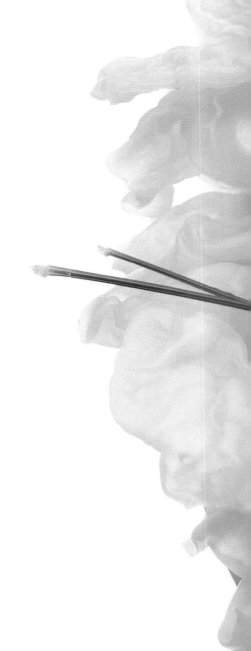

steaming

cabbage 'no nem'
spoon-style, with apples, pastrami and savora sauce

1 To make the Savora sauce, put the egg yolks in a bowl, season with salt and pepper and stir in both types of mustard. Slowly pour in a thin trickle of oil, whisking with a balloon whisk to make a very thick sauce. Add lemon juice to taste; this will thin it slightly. Set aside. **2** Remove the base of the cabbage and select 20 of the largest outer leaves. Cut out the cabbage heart. **3** Blanch 2 or 3 of the large leaves at a time in a large pan of boiling salted water. Drain and plunge immediately into iced water. Repeat with the cabbage heart, then drain again before shredding it. **4** Boil the unpeeled potatoes with the sea salt, garlic cloves, bay and thyme until tender. **5** Drain, leave until cool enough to handle then scoop the flesh from the skins. Mash the flesh coarsely in a large bowl. **6** Add the pastrami, apples, gherkins, veal and shredded cabbage heart to the bowl. Mix well, and season with salt and pepper. **7** Spread out 2 layers of catering-quality clingfilm. **8** Drain the cabbage leaves and cut out 20 discs about 12 cm in diameter. Place a disc on the clingfilm and put a spoonful of the potato mixture in the middle. Bring the clingfilm up and over the contents, folding the cabbage disc over the stuffing. Twist the clingfilm closed over the top. **9** Place the packages in a bamboo steamer. Steam for 8 minutes. **10** Serve accompanied by the Savora sauce.

serves 8–12: 32 ravioli   **ravioli dough:** 500 g strong white flour   generous 1/2 tsp salt
200 ml boiling water   40g lard   **filling:** 500 g finely chopped pork shoulder, cooked
32 peeled prawns   1 tsp garlic chilli sauce   soy sauce   slice fresh ginger, finely chopped
slice Japanese pickled ginger, finely chopped   juice of 1 large lemon   pepper
wines: United States: white Napa Valley 1997 Chardonnay Far Niente
France: Burgundy white 1998 Chablis Grand Cru Les Clos J.-P. Droin

steaming pork and prawn ravioli

1 To make the filling, mix together the pork, prawns, the garlic chilli sauce, a dash of soy sauce, both types of ginger, lemon juice and pepper. **2** To make the dough, put the flour and salt in a large bowl and make a well in the centre. Pour in the boiling water, add the lard and mix to a dough. **3** Immediately roll half the dough into a very thin sheet. **4** Cut out 32 discs with an 8 cm pastry cutter; place teaspoonfuls of filling (with 1 prawn per disc) on the discs. Roll out the remaining dough thinly, cut into discs and cover the others. Dampen the edges to seal. Alternatively, space mounds of filling on half the pastry, rolled out to a very large, thin sheet, cover with the other half and cut out and seal as for ravioli. **5** Steam in a bamboo steamer for at least 5 minutes until the dough is cooked. Season.

60

spicy tomato syrup 115

buttered baby spinach 134

sauce ▲   accompaniment ▲

Spoonfuls

serves 4: 1 slice of white bread   1 red pepper   1 green pepper   juice of 2 limes
1 chilli   1 shallot, finely sliced   1 garlic clove, finely chopped
very fresh sea bass fillet weighing 800 g   sea salt   pepper
wines: Italy: white Umbria 1997 Sauvignon-Chardonnay Conte della Vipera Antinori-de Ladoucette
France: Champagne Special Reserve Selected by Alain Ducasse Paul Drouet

spoonfuls

ceviche with grenoble relish and mimosa garnish

1 Cut the crusts from the bread and cut into thin strips. **2** Fry in a little oil until pale golden brown, then transfer to a sieve to drain. **3** Peel the peppers, discard the stalks, seeds and pith and dice finely. Add the lime juice, chilli, shallot and garlic. Add plenty of pepper. **4** Trim the fish fillet, then cut it into 1 cm thick slices. **5** Marinate each slice for only 10 seconds, just long enough to flavour it but not to 'cook', unlike classic ceviche. **6** Drain the fish then slice almost in half. Open out, like a book, and fill with the marinade, as a filling-cum-topping. Season with salt and pepper and garnish the plate with the mimosa. Serve the relish separately.

64

grenoble relish

▼ **sauce**

30 g butter
50 g capers
2 limes, divided into segments
1 slice of white bread, cut into very thin strips, fried

Heat the butter until golden brown, add the capers and cook for 1–2 minutes, then add the lime segments. Divide equally among 4 little sauce bowls and sprinkle with the fried bread strips.

mimosa

▼ **accompaniment**

2 hard-boiled eggs
small bunch of parsley

Separate the egg yolks from the whites. Push the yolks through a fine sieve and the whites through a coarser sieve, or chop finely. Chop the parsley very finely. Arrange in separate lines on each plate.

serves 4: 150 g Puy lentils   150 g black-eyed beans   150 g whole wheat grains
150 g spelt grains   150 g chickpeas   1/4 tsp raz-el-hanout (Moroccan spice mixture)
2 shallots, finely chopped   dash of sherry vinegar   2 pinches of mace
wines: Germany: white Baden 1997 Weissburgunder (Pinto blanc) Klassik Franz Keller
France: Burgundy white 1998 Burgundy Aligoté Bouzeron de Villaine

spoonfuls

cereals and pulses

1 Divide the flavouring ingredients into 5 portions (tie the cloves, thyme and bay leaves in muslin bags), and cook one portion with each separate type of pulse or grain: Puy lentils for 25–30 minutes; black-eyed beans for 1 1/2 hours; wheat as directed on packet; spelt grains for 45 minutes; chickpeas for 2 hours. Add salt only when each component is three-quarters cooked. **2** Drain off the cooking liquids into separate bowls. Discard the carrots, onions, pork and muslin bags. Return the grains and pulses to their saucepans, pour their stock over and leave to cool. Drain to serve. **3** Mix the raz-el-hanout into the chickpeas. **4** Mix the shallots with the wheat. **5** Sprinkle the sherry vinegar on to the Puy lentils. Mix the mace with the spelt. **6** Arrange the grains and pulses in a serving bowl, ideally in layers in a high-sided glass bowl, starting with the chickpeas. Serve at room temperature, handing round extra virgin olive oil, your favourite vinegar, sea salt and pepper.

66

flavourings: 200 g belly of pork or fat bacon, chopped   2 onions, sliced   2 carrots, sliced
4 cloves   3 sprigs of thyme   5 bay leaves   coarse sea salt   1.5 litres white stock (page 126)
to serve: extra virgin olive oil   your favourite vinegar – sherry, balsamic...   sea salt
coarsely ground black pepper

serves 4: spicy tomato coulis: 50 g sugar   1 tsp white wine vinegar or rice wine vinegar
2 large, ripe tomatoes, peeled   2 cm piece of fresh ginger, cut into fine strips
2 garlic cloves, finely chopped   dash of chilli sauce   dash of balsamic vinegar
wines: United States white Carneros 1997 Chardonnay Shafer
France: Burgundy white Côtes-de-Beaune 1998 Puligny Montrachet J.M. Boillot

Tempura of prawns and vegetables

spoonfuls

1 To make the tomato coulis, put the sugar and 1 1/4 tablespoons water in a small saucepan and cook until caramelized. Off the heat, add the wine vinegar; it will splutter. **2** Purée the tomatoes and add to the pan with the ginger, garlic, chilli sauce and balsamic vinegar. **3** To make the tempura batter, mix the flour, baking powder, salt and ground chilli. Add the oil and gradually beat in enough iced water, using a balloon whisk, to make a very smooth coating batter. **4** Cut the celery, spring onions, courgettes, fennel, asparagus and mushrooms into long, thin strips, 10 cm long and 1 cm wide. **5** Peel the prawns, make an incision along their backs and remove the black thread. **6** Dip the vegetables, courgette flowers and prawns in the batter, allowing the excess to drain off. **7** Half-fill a large pan with oil and heat to 180°C. Fry for 30 seconds. **8** Transfer to kitchen paper to drain. Sprinkle with sea salt and chilli pepper to taste. **9** To serve, arrange the vegetables in bunches, insert the rocket leaves among them and add the courgette flowers and prawns. **10** Serve the tomato sauce separately.

68

tempura batter: 100 g plain white flour   1/2 tsp baking powder   1 tsp salt   1/2 tsp mild chilli powder   1 tbsp olive oil   100 ml iced water
vegetables and seafood: 1 bunch of celery   4 large, fat spring onions   1 courgette   1 fennel bulb   4 green asparagus spears   50 g shiitake mushrooms   12 Mediterranean or tiger prawns   4 courgette flowers   sea salt   Espelette chilli powder   150 g rocket

serves 4: **cooked vegetables:** 1 small cauliflower   3 tbsp rice vinegar   mignonette pepper
250 g salsify   1 cardoon, stalks separated   3 Swiss chard stalks   1 turnip, sliced
200 g Jerusalem artichokes, sliced   1 bunch of white asparagus spears
250 g Japanese artichokes   3 tbsp soy sauce   **raw vegetables:** 1 black radish, sliced
1 bunch of enoki mushrooms   200 g shiitake mushrooms, thinly sliced   100 g soya bean sprouts
wines: South Africa: Stellenbosch 1997 Semillon Stellenzicht Reserve
France: Bordeaux white Côtes-de-Francs 1998 Château Les Charmes Godard

spoonfuls

medley of crisp and
tender white vegetables

1 Boil half the cauliflower in salted water; drain, purée and flavour with rice wine vinegar and mignonette pepper. **2** Boil the other vegetables separately in salted water until three-quarters done: the salsify for about 40 minutes; cardoons 30 minutes; Swiss chard stalks, turnip and artichokes 15 minutes; 10 minutes for the asparagus; Japanese artichokes 5 minutes; and the rest of the cauliflower, divided into florets, 3 minutes. **3** Drain each vegetable, refresh immediately and drain again. **4** Place all the vegetables in a wok and heat through while stirring and turning for 1 minute. **5** Add the raw vegetables and sprinkle with soy sauce and seasoning. Stir and turn briefly then transfer to a warmed covered casserole. **6** Serve with cauliflower purée and, when in season, red radishes and chicory.

1 For the cooked vegetables, cook half the broccoli florets in boiling salted water until tender. Drain then purée and season with pepper. **2** Cook the remaining broccoli and other vegetables separately in boiling salted water until three-quarters done: 2 minutes for the leeks; 2 minutes for mange touts and French beans; 3 minutes for the broccoli, haricot beans and okra. **3** Drain, refresh, and drain again. **4** Stir-fry with the raw vegetables in a wok for 2 minutes. **5** Mix all the vegetables together, add soy sauce to taste and stir and turn briefly before transferring to a warmed casserole. **6** Serve accompanied by the broccoli purée. Depending on the season, globe artichokes, young spinach, green cabbage and chicory can be added.

spoonfuls

medley of green vegetables

serves 4: **cooked vegetables:** 1 head of broccoli   salt   pepper   4 very thin baby leeks or young leek hearts   150 g mange tout   150 g French beans   150 g fresh haricot beans   8 okra olive oil   **raw vegetables:** 50 g Swiss chard leaves without stalks   Cos lettuce leaves, ribs removed   1/2 bunch flowering garlic chives   12 spring onions   4 garlic chives in bud
12 green asparagus spears, thinly sliced   salt   pepper   3 tbsp soy sauce
wines: Argentina: white Mendoza 1999 Torrontes
France: Alsace white 1998 Sylvaner Les Vieilles Vignes Ostertag

serves 4: 1.4 kg free-range chicken   olive oil   2 gelatine leaves   bunch of young carrots
16 round, red radishes   8 baby turnips, with their tops   100 g French beans
100 g shelled petits pois   100 g peeled baby broad beans   other vegetables newly in season –
broccoli, cauliflower, black radish   **consommé:** 1.5 litres white stock (page 126)   1 carrot
1 onion, halved and scorched on a griddle   1 bouquet garni   1 star anise   3 green cardamom pods
1/2 tsp coriander seeds   1/2 tsp black peppercorns   2 sprigs of tarragon

delicate chicken consommé, spring vegetables, 'chaudfroid' topping and crayfish

72

1 Detach and bone the chicken thighs and cut the fillets from the breast. Cook the thigh meat and fillets in a little oil for about 20 minutes without browning. Cut into 3 cm slices and set aside. **2** To make the consommé, put all the ingredients, the remainder of the chicken and giblets if available in a deep saucepan. Bring to the boil, remove the scum as it rises to the surface and boil gently until reduced by two thirds. Strain. Add 2 gelatine leaves to 150 ml water. Set aside. **3** To make the 'chaudfroid', boil the cream with the remaining broth until reduced. **4** Sweat each type of root vegetable separately with 1 tablespoon olive oil, and a little seasoning. Add water to half cover, cook, covered, until tender. **5** Boil the green vegetables separately in salted water until al dente. Drain and refresh. **6** To make the crayfish stock, cook the crayfish in boiling court bouillon for 4 minutes. Remove, drain, peel the tails only and reserve the heads and attached claws; to bring out their colour, fry in olive oil; remove and drain. **7** Use the same oil to cook the shallots, garlic, 1 sprig of tarragon and the celery then add the crayfish heads and claws and the tomato purée, cognac and the wine, flame and then continue cooking until reduced by half. Add just enough court bouillon to barely cover the ingredients and cook for 30 minutes. **8** Strain into a saucepan, pressing down firmly on the contents of the sieve. Add the remaining tarragon to the pan and simmer until well-flavoured and reduced to a fairly thick, syrupy consistency; it will be used to glaze the peeled crayfish tails and to add flavour to the jelly. **9** To serve, spoon a 1 cm deep layer of crayfish liquid in the bottom of a 10 cm high, 15 cm wide bowl, or 4 individual bowls. Cool completely, then add the vegetables and the chicken. Cover with the reserved consommé and chill until lightly set. **10** Spoon a 2 cm layer of the 'chaudfroid' on each portion and put the crayfish tails, glazed with some of the remaining crayfish liquid, on top.

'chaudfroid': 250 ml single cream   1 gelatine leaf, soaked and drained   1 sprig of tarragon
crayfish stock: 20 crayfish   250 ml court bouillon (page 126)   2 shallots   200 ml olive oil
3 garlic cloves   2 sprigs of tarragon   1/2 stick of celery   2 tbsp tomato purée
4 tbsp cognac   4 tbsp dry white wine
wines: United States white Monterey County 1994 Chardonnay Chalone Vineyards
France: Jura white 1996 L'Étoile-en-Mont-Genezet Domaine Voorhuis-Henquet

serves 4: 6 tbsp 'youm-koumg' soup (page 44)   pinch of sansho   3 scallops or 12 queen scallops
300 g carpet shell clams   300 g cockles   8 smooth venus clams   4 ormers (abalone)
8 peeled prawns   pinch of wasabi   50 g kombu, chopped   50 g samphire
wines: Italy: white Trentino Alto Adige 1995 Pinot gris-Chardonnay-Riesling-Viognier-Roussanne-Sémillon-Marsanne Contest Mitterberg Cason Hirschprunn
France: Bordeaux: white Graves 1997 Chântegrive

ormers with shellfish and kombu chilled bouillon with sansho

1 Flavour the soup with sansho and leave in a cold place until jellied. **2** See the recipe for 'youm-koumg' soup for cooking and opening the scallops, carpet shell clams and cockles. **3** Open the venus clams and detach the scarlet sections of flesh. Rinse very briefly and cut into thin strips, to be eaten raw. **4** Use a sharp-edged spoon to detach the ormer meat from the shells, reserving the shells. Discard the black parts from the ormers and cut the meat into matchstick strips. **5** Mix the wasabi into the kombu for the raw seaweed salad and use to line the ormer shells. Put the prepared seafood on top and cover with the jellied, sansho-flavoured 'youm-koung' soup. Garnish with the samphire and bright red venus clam meat. **6** Serve chilled.

e**gg**s

serves 4: 250 ml single cream   500 ml milk   1 star anise   1 bouquet garni (bay leaf, thyme, parsley, a small piece of celery)   500 g very fresh, thick, mid-section cod fillet   100 ml olive oil   2 garlic cloves, finely chopped   100 g flat leaf parsley, coarsely chopped   1 garlic clove, crushed   30 g butter   4 soft-boiled eggs   4 sprigs lamb's lettuce   1/2 tsp sherry vinegar   4 large slices white country bread
wines: Australia: white Eden Valley 1997 Sémillon Henschke "Louis"
France: Loire Valley white 1996 Pouilly Fumé-Cuvée Majorum Michel Redde & Fils

soft-boiled eggs with
buttered cod and brandade

1 Heat the cream and milk together until boiling point has just been reached. **2** Add the star anise and bouquet garni and leave to infuse for 15 minutes. **3** Poach 200 g of the cod in the milk for 5 minutes. Remove with a slotted spoon, draining well. **4** Break up the fish with a fork. Reserve 1 tablespoon of the olive oil and gradually beat the remainder into the cod until smooth to make the brandade, then add the chopped garlic and parsley. **5** Fry the remaining 300 g cod, and the garlic, in the butter and remaining oil, allowing 2 minutes on each side. **6** Take the cod fillet from the frying pan, reserving the butter, and gently separate the flesh into large flakes. **7** Place one quarter of the brandade on each plate, arrange the large cod flakes and soft-boiled eggs on top and garnish with some lamb's lettuce. **8** Add the sherry vinegar to the butter remaining in the frying pan, then spoon over each serving. Serve with the bread.

serves 4: 1 bunch of watercress   100 g baby spinach leaves   1 bunch of flat leaf parsley...
olive oil   3 garlic cloves, finely chopped   320 g fresh garlic   300 ml single cream   salt
pepper   200 g dried, smoked cod flakes   50 g rocket   50 g melted butter   8 soft-boiled eggs
wines: United States: white 1997 Chardonnay Hawk Crest Reserve Stag's Leap
France: Côtes-du-Rhône white 1997 Coudoulet de Beaucastel Perrin

soft-boiled eggs with dried cod flakes, garlic purée and fresh green sauce

eggs

1 To make the green sauce, remove the leaves from the watercress, spinach and parsley. Plunge into boiling salted water and immediately remove and refresh in a bowl of iced water to fix the colour. Reserve the blanching water. **2** Purée the leaves with a dash of olive oil and the chopped garlic cloves until smooth. If too thick, add a little of the blanching water. **3** Cut all but 2 of the fresh garlic cloves in half and discard any central shoots. Put into a pan, and cover with water, bring to the boil, then drain. Repeat this blanching once more with fresh cold water and then purée until smooth, gradually adding the cream. Season with salt and pepper. **4** Cut the remaining 2 garlic cloves into very thin strips, blanch them, pat dry and fry very briefly. Drain on kitchen paper. **5** Spoon some garlic purée into the centre of each plate and surround with a wide ribbon of green sauce. Add the cod flakes, the seasoned rocket, some melted butter, 2 eggs and a portion of the fried garlic pieces.

serves 4: 3 red peppers   olive oil   6 garlic cloves, finely chopped   2–3 sprigs of basil
12 tomatoes, skinned, halved, deseeded   salt   pepper   2 tsp caster sugar
3 sprigs of thyme   4 bay leaves   4 green tomatoes, skinned with a very sharp knife,
quartered, deseeded   5 basil leaves   Tabasco sauce   4 soft-boiled eggs   sea salt
2 thin slices of white bread, cut into fine strips, lightly browned in clarified butter
wines: United States: white Carneros 1997 Chardonnay Saintsbury
France: Burgundy white Côte Chalonnaise 1997 Pouilly fumé Mercurey Les Croichots
B. Lorenzon

cold soft-boiled egg
with tomatoes 3 ways

80

1 Quarter the peppers and put them in a small casserole with 100 ml olive oil, 4 garlic cloves and 2–3 sprigs of basil. Cover, and cook for 1 1/2–2 hours at 150°C/gas mark 2. **2** Place 12 tomato halves, cut side up, on an oiled baking sheet; sprinkle with salt, pepper, sugar and a little olive oil. Chop the remaining garlic and add that too, along with the thyme and bay leaves. **3** Put into as low an oven as possible and leave for about 3 hours to soften and partially dry. **4** Cut the remaining 12 tomato halves lengthwise in three and season with salt and pepper. **5** Use a small, very sharp knife to peel off the thin skin from the peppers and slice the flesh into thin strips. **6** Transfer the peppers, slow-baked tomatoes, fresh tomatoes and green tomatoes to a salad bowl. **7** Add the basil leaves, snipped into small pieces, a few drops of Tabasco sauce and more seasoning if wished. **8** Arrange on wide, fairly deep dishes, placing an egg in the centre of each and top with the sea salt, pepper and fried bread strips.

serves 4: 2 bunches of very thick green asparagus spears   3 whole eggs   150 ml single cream   salt   pepper   4 soft-boiled eggs   1/2 bunch of watercress   1/2 tsp dried wakame
citrus sauce: juice of 1 orange   juice of 1/2 grapefruit   juice of 1/2 mandarin   juice of 1/2 lime   2 tbsp light soy sauce   2 tbsp rice wine vinegar   20 g dried bonito flakes
wines: United States: white Napa Valley 1997 Chardonnay Private Reserve Beringer
France: Burgundy: white Cotes-de-Beaune 1998 Puligny-Montrachet Carillon

eggs

soft-boiled eggs
with seared and raw asparagus spears and citrus sauce

82

1 Two or three days before planning to serve the dish, make the citrus sauce by mixing all the ingredients together. Leave to stand for a couple of hours, then strain through a fine non-metallic sieve. Store in a cool place until required. **2** Cut the top 10 cm off the asparagus spears and cook half of these in boiling salted water for 1–2 minutes. Drain, refresh in iced water. Drain again and set aside. **3** Using a mandolin, cut the remaining spears into long thin slivers. **4** Steam the stalks until tender, refresh in iced water, drain and purée. **5** Push the purée through a fine sieve and set aside to cool. **6** Beat in the raw eggs and cream. Season with salt and pepper to taste. **7** Pour into 4 heatproof bowls and cook in a bain-marie in a preheated oven at 180°C/gas mark 4 for about 20 minutes until lightly set. **8** Cook the reserved blanched asparagus on a hot griddle, or in a heavy frying pan until lightly browned. Transfer to a plate and sprinkle with some of the citrus sauce and then with dried wakame. **9** Repeat with the slivers of raw asparagus. Remove the asparagus custards from the oven and put a soft-boiled egg on top. **10** Arrange the cooked and raw asparagus and watercress sprigs around the eggs and add the remaining citrus sauce. Sprinkle with wakame.

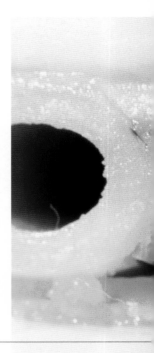

pasta

serves 6: 30 g butter   3 tbsp olive oil   400 g artisan dried macaroni
1 litre white stock (page 126)   salt   pepper
wines: Italy: red Piedmont 1995 Nebbiolo Valmaggiore Sandrone
France: Bordeaux red 1999 Château Mouton

pasta

Connoisseur's
macaroni

1 Heat the butter and olive oil in a large, deep saucepan and stir in the macaroni for 1 minute. **2** Gradually add the hot stock, stirring continually with a wooden spoon, as when making risotto. **3** The pasta should take 15–18 minutes to cook. **4** Add your choice of finishing touch: lean ham cut into fine strips, slivers of fresh truffle, a little pesto...

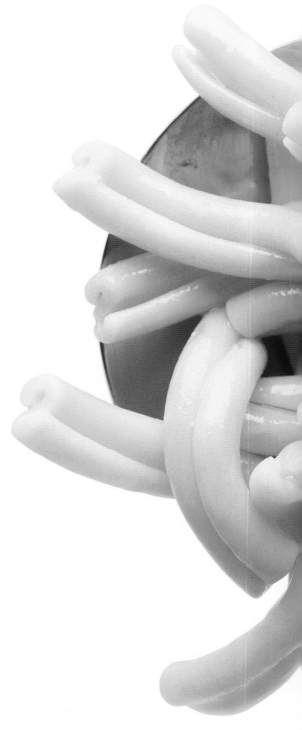

86

parmesan
strips of ham
grated gruyère cheese

▼ **sauce**   ▲ **accompaniment**

compote of tomatoes 3 ways

60 g spring onions
50 ml olive oil
260 g skinned deseeded and
coarsely chopped tomatoes
5 g finely chopped garlic
large pinch of sea salt
110 g long strips of skinned tomato
55 g slow-baked tomatoes
(step 2, page 80) cut into fine strips
25 g sun-dried tomatoes, puréed
dash of Tabasco sauce

Sweat the sliced spring onions in the oil, add the chopped tomatoes, the garlic and salt. Cover and cook very gently over the lowest possible heat for 2 hours, stirring occasionally. Leave to cool, then stir in the remaining ingredients.

serves 4: about 500 ml whole milk   500 ml single cream   pinch of grated nutmeg
3 garlic cloves   1 bay leaf   1 sprig of thyme   salt   pepper   500 g macaroni, preferably straight
30 g butter   30 g plain flour   100 g mature Cheddar or Gouda cheese, very thinly sliced
wines: Spain: red Rioja 1996 Remelluri
France: Burgundy white Cote-de-Nuits 1997 Marsannay P. Nadeff

pasta

baked
macaroni cheese

1 Pour the milk and cream into a fairly deep and wide, heavy-bottomed saucepan and add the nutmeg, garlic, bay leaf, thyme, salt and pepper. Bring to a simmer and leave to reduce for 15 minutes. **2** Add the macaroni, cover and cook until just tender, then remove with a slotted spoon. Strain then measure the liquid: 550 ml is needed; add more milk and cream if necessary. Return to the pan, off the heat. **3** Heat the butter in a small, heavy-bottomed saucepan and stir in the flour using a balloon whisk to make a roux. **4** Whisk into the milk, return to the heat and bring to the boil, whisking. Simmer for 4–5 minutes to make a béchamel sauce. **5** Spread the macaroni in a single, tightly-packed layer without any spaces, in a large shallow dish. **6** Pour about half the sauce evenly over the macaroni to cover completely. Leave to cool. **7** When cold, use a 10 cm plain cutter to cut out 8 discs from the macaroni. **8** Put a disc in each of 4 individual ovenproof dishes and cover with thinly sliced cheese. Spoon on a layer of béchamel. Cover with another disc and finish with a layer of cheese. **9** Bake in a preheated oven at 200°C/gas mark 6 for 15 minutes. For a larger portion, you can double the height of the macaroni stack, as shown opposite.

shortcut: **6** Spread half the macaroni in a single layer in an ovenproof dish. **7** Cover with a layer of béchamel sauce and then with a layer of cheese slices. Repeat. Bake as above for 15 minutes.

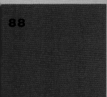

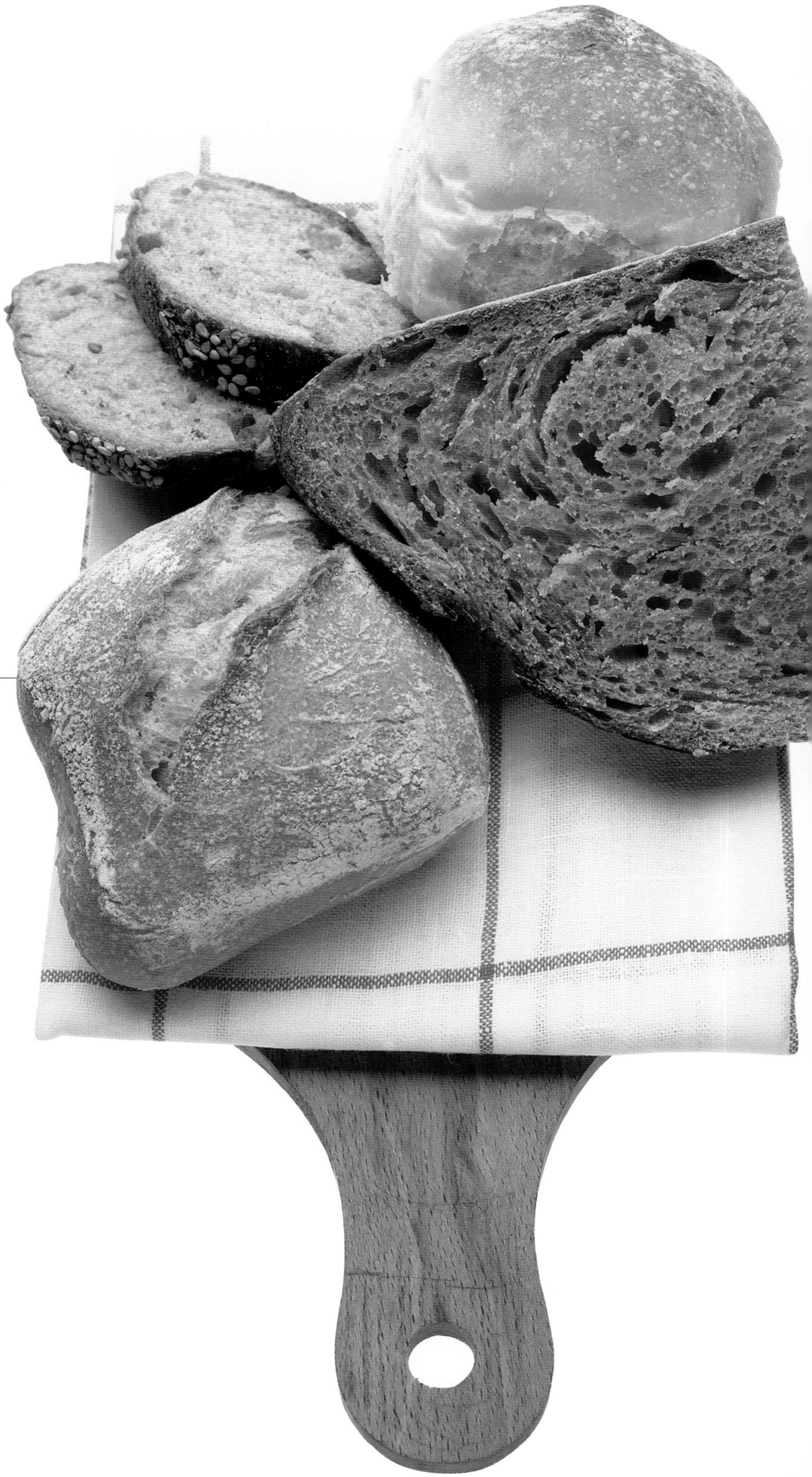

sandwiches

serves 4: 600 g very fresh tuna cut from the belly and back   sea salt   pepper   olive oil   1/2 tsp ground chillies   4 garlic cloves   200 g baby spinach leaves   4 large slices of white country bread, toasted   **mushroom duxelles:** 1 shallot, finely chopped   20 g butter   1 tsp olive oil   300 g mixed shiitake and button mushrooms, finely chopped   1 garlic clove, finely chopped   1/2 teaspoon chopped chervil   1/2 tsp finely chopped tarragon   1/2 tsp finely chopped parsley
wines: **United States:** white   Santa Barbara-Santa Maria   1997   **Italy:** Tocai Friulano   Borgo Buon Natale   **France:** Provence   white   Côtes-de-Provence   1998   Château Sainte-Marguerite

toro-tuna seared tuna, spinach and mushroom open sandwich

1 Cover the belly cut of tuna with plenty of coarse sea salt and leave in a cool place for 3 hours. Rinse off the salt, dry the tuna then marinate in 3 tablespoons olive oil, the ground chillies and 3 crushed garlic cloves. **2** To make the piperade, sweat the finely sliced onion and add the finely diced peppers, the crushed garlic cloves, the tomatoes and basil. Cover and cook gently for 30 minutes.

3 To make the duxelles, sweat the shallot in the butter and oil, add the mushrooms and leave to cook gently, uncovered, until the moisture has evaporated. Add the garlic and herbs, cook a little longer, then set aside. **4** Discard the stalks from the spinach and mix the leaves with a little olive oil and seasoning. **5** Rub the toast with the cut surfaces of the remaining garlic clove, spread a layer of the mushroom duxelles about 5 mm thick over the surface and cover with a thin layer of spinach. **6** Just before serving, sear the tuna over its entire surface and cut lengthwise into slices about 5 mm thick. Place on the spinach, cover with the piperade and season with salt and pepper.

piperade topping: 1 small onion or a large spring onion   1 red pepper   1 green pepper
6 garlic cloves   2 tomatoes, skinned, deseeded and chopped   1 sprig of basil

serves 8: 2 round lettuce hearts   2 red oak leaf lettuce hearts   2 red radicchio or Treviso chicory hearts   2 Cos lettuce hearts   vinaigrette (page 97)   pepper   sea salt
hummus: 150 g chickpeas, soaked overnight in cold water   1/2 tsp raz-el-hanout
50 ml sesame oil   salt   pepper   juice of 1/2 lemon   1/2 tsp paprika
tzatziki: 2 cucumbers   juice of 1 lemon   100 g thick yogurt, drained in a muslin-lined sieve for 30 minutes   salt   pepper   1/2 tsp finely chopped mint
courgette compote: 5 small courgettes (yellow or green)   white part of 1 spring onion, cut into rings   olive oil   salt   pepper   2 garlic cloves, partially crushed in their skins
5 sprigs of marjoram   marjoram leaves   **aubergine caviar:** 4 long, thin aubergines
8 garlic cloves   salt   pepper   50 ml olive oil   4 sprigs of thyme   1 shallot   10 basil leaves
wines: United States: white Sonoma Valley 1997 Sauvignon blanc Rochioli
France: Bordeaux white Côtes-de-Francs 1998 Château Les Charmes Godard

crunchy salad snacks

1 To make the hummus, drain the chickpeas. **2** Put into a saucepan with clean water and bring to the boil. Add the raz-el-hanout and boil gently for 2 hours until tender. Rinse in cold water and leave to cool. Crush to a purée. **3** Gradually beat the oil into the chickpeas. Season with salt and pepper. **4** Add the lemon juice and paprika. **5** To make the tzatziki, peel off the cucumber skin in alternate strips (page 12); cut in half lengthwise and scoop out the seeds. **6** Chop the cucumbers finely and put in a sieve to drain for 1 hour. **7** Combine the cucumber with the lemon juice, drained yogurt, seasoning and mint.
8 To make the courgette compote, slice the courgettes in half lengthwise and discard any seeds. **9** Purée the courgettes. Fry the spring onion very gently in a little olive oil in a sauté pan and stir in the courgettes. Add the seasoning, garlic and marjoram. **10** Cook over a fairly high heat for 10 minutes, then half-submerge the pan in iced water to cool it completely and ensure the compote keeps its colour.
11 Remove the marjoram and garlic, and add marjoram leaves to taste. **12** To make the aubergine caviar, cut incisions in the aubergines and insert slivers of garlic. **13** Place on large sheets of foil, season with salt and pepper; brush liberally with olive oil and add the thyme. Fold over the foil loosely and seal the edges tightly. **14** Bake in a preheated oven at 200°C/gas mark 6 for 1 1/2 hours until very tender.
15 Leave to cool before scooping out the flesh with a spoon. Mix the flesh with the chopped shallot and basil and more seasoning if wished.
16 Once all the toppings are ready, slice the salad hearts in half lengthwise and sprinkle with a little vinaigrette. **17** Top each heart with a spoonful of one of one of the toppings. Place a rounded spoonful of each topping on each plate and put a heart with the matching topping on top. **18** Season with a grind of pepper and sprinkling of sea salt just before serving.

serves 4: 4 slices of white country bread, about 20 cm long and 1.5 cm thick
1 garlic clove   4 tbsp tapenade   3 tbsp pesto   3 tbsp tomato compote
16 slices of smoked bacon   8 slices of pancetta, about 15 cm long
6 little gem lettuce hearts, halved lengthwise   vinaigrette (page 97)
24 slices of slow-baked tomatoes (step 2, page 80)   bacon salt (page 97)

b.l.t
bacon, lettuce and tomato
open sandwich

1 To make the pesto, crush the garlic with a pestle and mortar then add the basil leaves and pound to a smooth paste. Transfer to a bowl and beat in the olive oil, adding a little at a time. Pound the pine nuts in the mortar and add to the bowl with the Parmesan. Mix well. **2** To make the bacon salt, bake the bacon in a fairly hot oven until crisp and dry, then process to a powder. **3** To make the vinaigrette, whisk together the vinegar, oil and seasoning. Sprinkle over the lettuce hearts. **4** To make the tomato compote, thoroughly mix together the 3 types of tomatoes. **5** Toast the bread on one side only then rub this side with the cut surfaces of the garlic clove. **6** Spread the tapenade, pesto and tomato compote in 3 bands of red, black and green along the length of each slice of toast, garlic side uppermost. **7** Grill the 16 bacon slices and the pancetta and wipe off surplus fat with kitchen paper. **8** Cover part of each band of topping with a lettuce heart, drizzle with vinaigrette and top with baked tomato, bacon and pancetta. Sprinkle with the bacon salt and serve immediately.

pesto: 3 garlic cloves   1 bunch of basil   150 ml olive oil   50 g pine nuts
2 tbsp freshly and finely grated Parmesan cheese
bacon salt: 4 slices of smoked streaky bacon
vinaigrette: 1 tbsp sherry vinegar   3 tbsp olive oil   salt   pepper
tomato compote: 1 tbsp cooked tomato concassé   1 tbsp sun-dried tomatoes
1 tbsp chopped slow-baked tomatoes (step 2, page 80)
wines: Italy: white   Lombardy   1996   Chardonnay   Ca' Del Bosco
France: Côtes-du-Rhone   red   Vin des Pays des Collines Rhodaniennes
La Sérine Pointue   Colombo

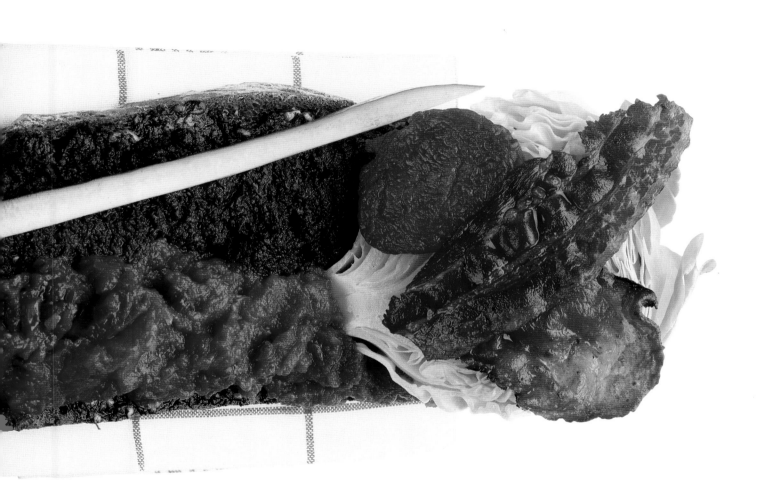

1 To make the mustard mayonnaise, mix the mustard with the egg yolks then slowly pour in the oil, whisking continuously. Season. 2 Slice 20 discs from the largest cabbage leaves, using a 10 cm diameter pastry cutter. 3 Remove the ribs from the remaining cabbage and shred finely. Mix into the mustard mayonnaise with the gherkins and set aside. 4 Warm the pastrami in the white stock in a bain marie. 5 Place a cabbage disc on each of 4 warmed plates. Spoon a layer of mayonnaise filling on top and cover with a slice of drained pastrami. Repeat four more times. 6 Toast the bread on one side, remove the crusts and slice into strips 3 cm wide. Arrange one quarter of the toast around each layered 'sandwich'. 7 Shortcut: use cold pastrami.

sandwiches

pastrami with toast soldiers

serves 4: 1 Chinese cabbage   2 sweet-sour gherkins, cut into rounds
20 slices pastrami   250 ml white stock (page 126)   4 slices of white country bread
mustard mayonnaise: 1 1/2 tsp Savora mustard   2 egg yolks   250 ml groundnut oil
salt   pepper

1 See toro-tuna, page 92 for the preparation of the tuna. Skin, deseed and slice the peppers and tomatoes. Mix then chill until needed. 2 Whisk the vinaigrette ingredients together. 3 To make the topping, in a bowl, mix the egg yolks with the mustard, chilli powder and lemon juice. Gradually beat in the oil to make a very thick mayonnaise. Fold in the remaining ingredients. 4 Put 3 lines of topping on each plate. 5 Cut the lettuces in half, drizzle with the vinaigrette and add to the plates. 6 Season the tomato mixture and put on the salads. 7 Sear the tuna evenly, thinly slice and add to the salads with the French beans.

bagnat salad

serves 4: 1 red pepper   1 green pepper   1 yellow pepper   2 tomatoes   2 red oak leaf or round lettuces   300 g belly cut of fresh tuna   100 g blanched French beans   **topping:** 2 egg yolks   2 tbsp Dijon mustard   pinch of chilli powder   juice of 1 lemon   40 ml oil   2 hard-boiled eggs, finely chopped   50 g capers   2 salted anchovies, finely chopped   1/2 tsp chopped parsley   1 spring onion, sliced   **sherry vinaigrette:**   1 tbsp sherry vinegar   3 tbsp olive oil   salt   pepper   **wines: Italy** white Veneto 1997 Soave Capitel Foscarini Anselmi   **France:** Côtes-du-Rhône white 1997 Coudoulet de Beaucastel Perrin

3

sauces

serves 4: 1 kg long, thin aubergines   60 ml olive oil   100 g chestnut flower honey
5 small, very hot chillies   2 tbsp mustard seeds   20 g peppercorns
1/2 tsp finely grated fresh ginger   1/2 tsp turmeric   1 tbsp cumin seeds   3 bay leaves
150 ml lemon juice   3 tbsp fine salt   a few briefly-fried fine aubergine strips

sweet-sour
aubergine pickle

1 Peel off alternate strips of aubergine skin (see cucumber photograph on page 12). Slice lengthwise into pieces 2 cm thick and then cut into 2 cm cubes. **2** Fry in the oil in a frying pan until brown. Transfer to a colander to drain. **3** Heat the honey in a saucepan over a low heat with the coarsely crushed chillies, mustard seeds, peppercorns, ginger, turmeric, cumin, bay leaves and aubergine cubes. Stir and turn carefully, then mix in the lemon juice. **4** Simmer gently for 20 minutes. Discard the bay leaves, season with salt and stir in the fried aubergine strips.

102

1 Peel the raw beetroot and cut it into thin strips. Peel the baked beetroot and dice it finely. 2 Warm the diced beetroot gently in a pan with the honey, mace and chopped chillies; then stir in the vinegar. 3 Leave to cook, uncovered, until the vinegar has reduced by half. Add the strips of beetroot season with salt and pepper and cook while stirring for about 30 seconds until the consistency resembles that of a compote. 4 Transfer to a dish and leave to cool.

beetroot pickle

sauces

serves 4: 1 large raw beetroot   1 large baked beetroot
(ideally, cooked in foil in glowing embers)   2 tbsp honey   1/2 tsp ground mace
2 bird's eye chillies   100 ml wine vinegar   salt   pepper

serves 4: 25 g coarsely chopped peeled walnuts
mustard vinaigrette: 1 tbsp white vinegar   3 tbsp olive oil   2 tbsp peanut oil   salt   pepper
1 tbsp traditional coarse-grain mustard   1 shallot, sliced into thin rings

sauces

walnut relish

1 To make the mustard vinaigrette, whisk together the vinegar, oils, salt, pepper and mustard. Add the shallot.
2 Stir in the walnuts.

genoese pesto
sauces

1 Using a pestle and mortar, pound the garlic, basil leaves and oil to a paste. **2** Work in the Parmesan and the pine nuts.

105

1 Remove the leaves from the basil sprigs then pound them to a paste with the rocket, oil and garlic using a pestle and mortar. **2** Season with salt and pepper.

herb pesto
sauces

1 bunch of basil   100 g rocket   100 ml olive oil
6 garlic cloves   sea salt   pepper

serves 4: 1 green mango   salt   200 ml rice wine vinegar   2 bird's eye chillies
75 g brown cane sugar   25 g chopped spring onions (white part only)
2 garlic cloves, finely chopped   50 g raisins   60 g flaked, toasted almonds
150 g ripe mango flesh, cut into fine strips   2 basil leaves, finely chopped
25 g fresh ginger, finely chopped   30 g Japanese pickled ginger

sauces ⌐mango **chutney**

1 The day before you plan to serve the chutney, cut the green mango into 5 mm dice, sprinkle with salt and leave in a colander over a bowl overnight to release their moisture. Rinse, drain and pat dry with kitchen paper. **2** In a fairly deep, non-aluminium frying pan, boil the vinegar with the chillies and sugar. Add the spring onions, garlic and diced mango. **3** Cook for 10 minutes then add the raisins and leave to cool. **4** Stir in the almonds, the strips of ripe mango, the basil and both types of ginger. **5** The relish should be like a compote in consistency.

106

serves 4: 200 g ripe, unwaxed, smooth-skinned lemons
90 g caster sugar   60 ml lemon juice

lemon relish

sauces

1 Remove the zest from the lemons in strips and cut the strips into short lengths. Cook gently with half the sugar and all the lemon juice. **2** Remove the pith from the lemons and segment the flesh. Cook gently with the remaining sugar for about 1 hour. **3** Mix the zest and flesh.

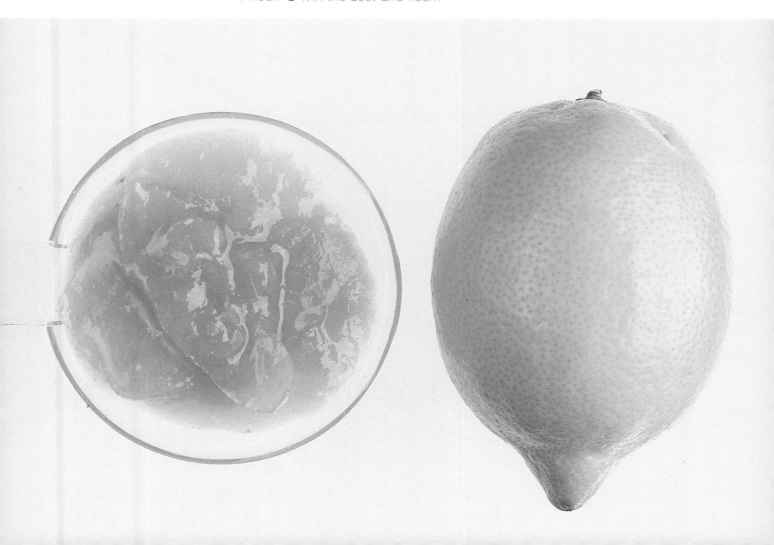

serves 4: 2 salted anchovies   2 spring onions
10 black olives, pitted   2 tbsp tapenade
about 4 tbsp of sherry vinaigrette
(see bagnat salad, page 99)

sauces

ancholive

1 Rinse the anchovies. Remove the backbones and cut the fillets into thin strips. Chop the spring onions and the olives coarsely. **2** Spoon the tapenade into a bowl and stir in sherry vinaigrette to taste. **3** Add the anchovies, spring onions and olives.

108

1 Mix the egg yolks with the mustard then gradually add the oil, whisking continuously. Season and stir in the lemon. **2** Remove the oysters from their shells, chop the flesh and add to the mayonnaise along with the clams and herbs.

sauces

oyster and lemon dressing

serves 4: 2 egg yolks   1 tbsp Dijon mustard   250 ml olive oil   juice of 2 lemons
4 very fresh oysters   2 tbsp very small raw clams   1/2 tsp chervil, finely chopped
1/2 tsp chives, finely chopped

serves 4: 1 egg yolk   1 tbsp Dijon mustard
100 ml grapeseed oil   60 g freshly grated horseradish root
2 tbsp crème fraîche   pepper   salt   celery salt

horseradish sauce

sauces

1 Mix the egg yolk with the mustard then gradually whisk in the oil. Stir in the horseradish, followed by the crème fraîche. **2** Add pepper, salt and celery salt to taste.

109

1 To make the green sauce, briefly fry the spinach, watercress and parsley in the oil with the chopped garlic. **2** Transfer to a deep bowl and cool quickly by half-immersing the bowl in iced water to retain the green colour. **3** Purée with the stock. **4** Cut the ginger into thin strips and shred the remaining leaves and herbs finely. Fold into the green sauce.

ginger and herb relish

sauces

serves 4: large piece of fresh ginger   5 borage leaves   50 g rocket
10 sorrel leaves   5 basil leaves   green sauce: 150 g spinach leaves
1/2 bunch of watercress   1/2 bunch of flat leaf parsley   olive oil
3 garlic cloves   100 ml white stock (page 126)   salt   pepper

serves 4: 800 g very young peas in the pod   2 tbsp olive oil
500 g baby broad beans in the pod   2 spring onions
tips of 4 green asparagus spears   salt   pepper   chives

spring relish

1 Shell the peas and reserve 2 tablespoons. Cook the remainder in boiling salted water, drain and purée until very smooth. **2** Blanch the reserved peas briefly, cool immediately in iced water, drain and carefully remove the thin skins. **3** Remove the broad beans from their pods. Squeeze the beans gently to pop them out of their skins. Chop the spring onions finely. Cut the asparagus tips into thin slivers. **4** Stir the whole, skinned peas, spring onions and the broad beans into the purée and adjust the seasoning. Spoon into 4 small saucers and sprinkle with chives and slivers of asparagus.

serves 4: 200 g caster sugar   250 ml fresh orange juice   1 tbsp balsamic vinegar
250 ml sherry vinegar   1 sprig of rosemary   1 garlic clove   10 fresh, ripe tomatoes
1 tbsp sun-dried tomatoes   dash of Tabasco sauce   salt   pepper

sauces

sweet/acid tomato sauce

1 Mix 100 g of sugar with 3 tablespoons water and cook until pale golden-brown in a small, heavy-bottomed saucepan to make a light caramel. **2** Stir in the orange juice, both types of vinegar, the rosemary and garlic. **3** Leave off the heat to allow the flavours to mingle for 10 minutes. Strain and set aside. **4** Purée the tomatoes with the remaining ingredients then pass through a sieve. **5** Combine equal volumes of these two flavoured liquids, stirring well. Season with salt and pepper.

112

1 Cook 4 asparagus spears in boiling salted water until tender. **2** Refresh in iced water, drain and purée with the olive oil. Pass through a fine sieve and stir in the concentrated chicken juices. **3** Cut the tips of the remaining asparagus spears into quarters and cook briefly over a gentle heat in a heavy-bottomed saucepan to dry-roast them. **4** Chop the asparagus spears and cook them with a very little water. **5** Slice the shallots into rings and fry them. **6** Add the cooked asparagus into the purée and sprinkle with the dry-roast tips and the fried shallots.

sauces

asparagus relish

serves 4: 8 asparagus spears   1–2 tbsp olive oil
1 tbsp cooking juices from a roast chicken   2 shallots

serves 4: 2 boned chicken legs   3 garlic cloves   1 1/2 green apples, finely chopped   50 g fresh ginger, chopped   1–2 bird's eye chillies   generous pinch of ground mace   generous pinch of ground ginger   6 green cardamom pods   pinch of ground chilli   1 litre concentrated chicken stock (page 126)   3 small pots of plain yogurt, drained overnight in a muslin-lined sieve   juice of 1/2 lime   1 tbsp chopped coriander leaves   1/2 tsp finely chopped fresh ginger

tandoori sauce

1 Chop the skinned chicken and brown in a heavy-bottomed saucepan. **2** Add the garlic, one third of the apples, the ginger and the spices. **3** Add enough chicken stock to cover and simmer, uncovered, removing any scum from the surface as it rises. **4** Strain through a conical sieve and then continue cooking, uncovered, until the liquid has reduced to syrupy consistency. Leave to cool. **5** When cold, stir in the yogurt, remaining apple, lime juice, coriander and the chopped ginger.

1 Pour the coconut milk into a wide, fairly deep saucepan, add the lemon grass, vanilla and ginger. Simmer until reduced to a thick sauce, then strain through a conical sieve. **2** While still hot, add the diced mango, apple, lemon balm, mint and chilli powder, and salt and pepper to taste. **3** Leave to cool before stirring in the lobster coral and tomalley.

lemon grass sauce

serves 4: 400 ml coconut milk   1 lemon grass bulb   1/2 vanilla pod   4 thin slices of fresh ginger   100 g diced green mango   100 g diced ripe mango   100 g diced Granny Smith apple   5 lemon balm leaves, cut into thin strips   5 mint leaves, cut into thin strips   1/2 tsp chilli powder (preferably hot)   salt   pepper   coral of 1 lobster   tomalley (liver) of 1 lobster

sauces

satay sauce

1 Heat the olive oil, add the curry paste and stir well then stir in the peanut paste, sugar and vinegar. **2** Bring to the boil and stir in the creamed coconut. **3** Simmer until small droplets of oil rise to the surface, remove from the heat and process with a hand-held mixer.

114

serves 4: 500 g ripe tomatoes   80 g caster sugar   1 tsp mignonette pepper
10 g salt   100 ml olive oil   500 ml tomato juice   6 garlic cloves
1/2 bunch of basil   2 tbsp chilli sauce   1 tbsp Tabasco sauce

spicy tomato syrup

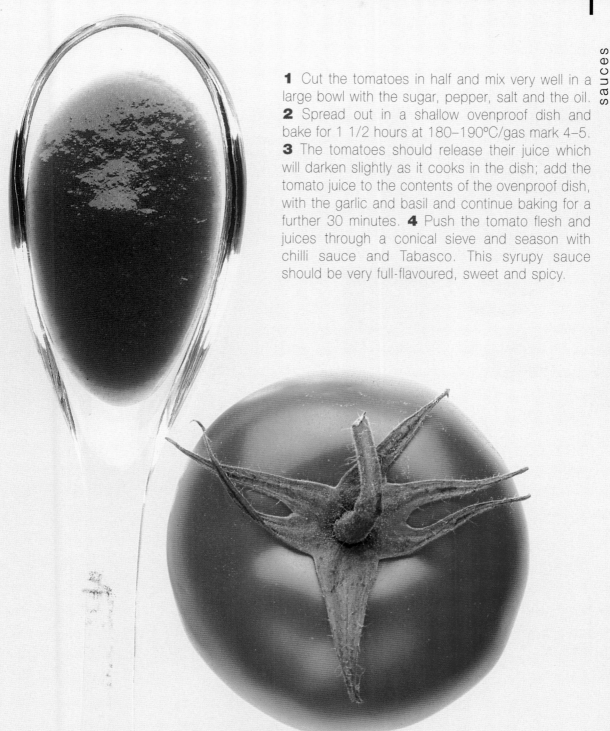

sauces

1 Cut the tomatoes in half and mix very well in a large bowl with the sugar, pepper, salt and the oil. **2** Spread out in a shallow ovenproof dish and bake for 1 1/2 hours at 180–190ºC/gas mark 4–5. **3** The tomatoes should release their juice which will darken slightly as it cooks in the dish; add the tomato juice to the contents of the ovenproof dish, with the garlic and basil and continue baking for a further 30 minutes. **4** Push the tomato flesh and juices through a conical sieve and season with chilli sauce and Tabasco. This syrupy sauce should be very full-flavoured, sweet and spicy.

115

serves 4: 4 tsp olive oil   150 g chopped spring onions   15 g mustard seeds
250 ml dry white wine   thyme flowers   1 bay leaf   5 g sea salt
generous pinch of mignonette pepper   1/4 litre white stock (page 126)   10 g Meaux mustard
30 g Dijon mustard   60 g gherkins, cut into very fine matchstick strips   juice of 1 lemon

sauces

gherkin and onion mustard relish

1 Heat the olive oil in a fairly deep frying pan and gently fry the spring onions and mustard seeds. **2** Add the white wine, stir and leave to simmer, uncovered, to reduce. **3** Add the thyme, bay leaf, sea salt, pepper and the white stock. Continue simmering until the sauce has thickened considerably. **4** Remove from the heat; stir in the Meaux and Dijon mustards, the gherkins and the lemon juice.

116

1 Cut the beef into large 5 cm cubes; brown these all over in olive oil in a large, heavy-bottomed saucepan. Remove the meat from the pan and set aside. **2** Add the onions, carrot, celery and garlic to the pan and cook gently. Return the meat, add the red wine and cook, uncovered, until the liquid has reduced by half. **3** Remove the zest from the orange and cut it into short, thin strips. Add the whole orange, bouquet garni, clove, pepper, orange juice and veal stock. Leave to simmer at length before draining off the remaining, concentrated liquid (about 800 ml). **4** Stir in the orange zest and the stoned and chopped olives. **5** Add salt and pepper to taste.

sauces

savoury orange sauce

serves 4–6: 500 g braising steak   2 tbsp olive oil   2 onions   1 carrot   1 celery stalk
3 garlic cloves, partially crushed but still whole   1 litre dry red wine   1 small orange
1 bouquet garni   1 clove   generous pinch of mignonette pepper   250 ml freshly-squeezed
orange juice   500 ml veal stock (page 126)   2 tbsp olives   salt   pepper

serves 4: 2 tbsp olive oil   1 tablespoon red curry paste
150 g unsalted roast peanuts   3 tbsp honey   8 garlic cloves   100 ml wine vinegar
250 ml concentrated stock (page 126)   1 tbsp smooth peanut butter
400 ml   coconut milk   3 spring onions, chopped
1 tbsp chopped roast peanuts

peanut sauce

sauces

1 Heat the olive oil and the curry paste in a deep frying pan. **2** Add the peanuts, 2 tablespoons honey, 2 crushed garlic cloves and the wine vinegar. **3** Stir and leave to simmer until reduced by half. Add the concentrated stock and peanut butter. Simmer briefly before straining through a conical sieve. **4** Tip the contents of the conical sieve into a saucepan, add the coconut milk and simmer until the milk has thickened considerably. Purée the sauce with the remaining honey. At this point the sauce can be used to coat spare ribs of pork. **5** Cut the remaining garlic into thin slices and fry until lightly coloured, remove and set aside. Fry the chopped spring onions. **6** Add the fried garlic, the spring onions and chopped peanuts to the sauce.

117

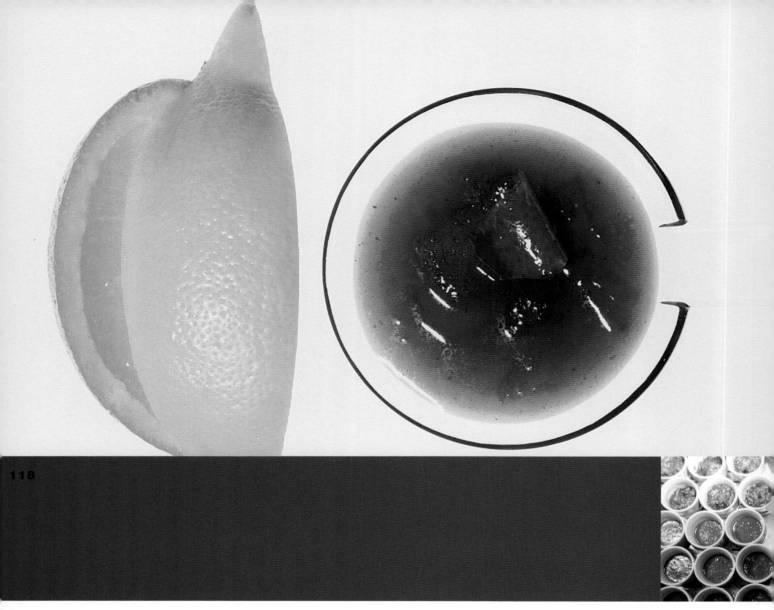

1 Place the sugar and 20 ml water in a small, heavy-bottomed saucepan and boil until caramelized. Remove from the heat. Add the citrus juices and the wine vinegar. **2** Return to the heat and simmer, uncovered, to reduce considerably before adding the duck stock. **3** Reduce again until somewhat thicker. Add the twice-blanched orange and lemon zests, the pepper and a dash of sherry vinegar.

sauces

bigarade sauce

serves 4: 50 g sugar   juice and zest of 1 orange   juice and zest of 1 lemon
100 ml wine vinegar   200 ml concentrated duck stock (page 126)
1/2 tsp mignonette pepper   dash of sherry vinegar

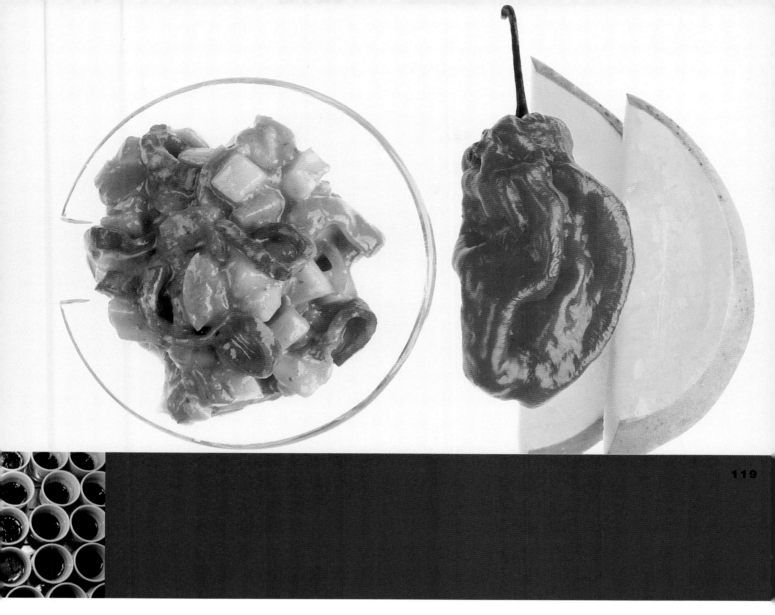

1 Fry the onions gently in the olive oil, add 2 of the chillies, finely chopped and the chilli paste. **2** Add the slivers of garlic and continue frying gently. **3** Add the reduced and thickened coconut milk. **4** Once the sauce has thickened further, add the mangoes, the remaining chilli cut into slivers and adjust the seasoning to taste.

mango and chilli relish sauces

serves 4: 2 red onions, finely chopped   2 tbsp olive oil   3 Scotch bonnet chillies
1/2 tsp chilli paste   8 garlic cloves, cut into thin strips
400 ml coconut milk, simmered to reduce by half
100 g diced ripe mango   100 g diced green mango   salt   pepper

serves 4: 1/2 tsp yellow curry paste   100 ml olive oil   100 g diced squid
400 ml coconut milk   5 Thai basil leaves, chopped   1 Granny Smith apple, diced
6 spring onions, chopped   salt   pepper

curry sauce

1 Stir the curry paste into the oil over a moderate heat in a fairly deep frying pan, then add the diced squid and fry gently. **2** Pour in the coconut milk and simmer until reduced and thickened considerably. **3** Remove from the heat and leave until cold. Stir in the basil leaves, the apple and the spring onions. **4** Adjust the seasoning to taste.

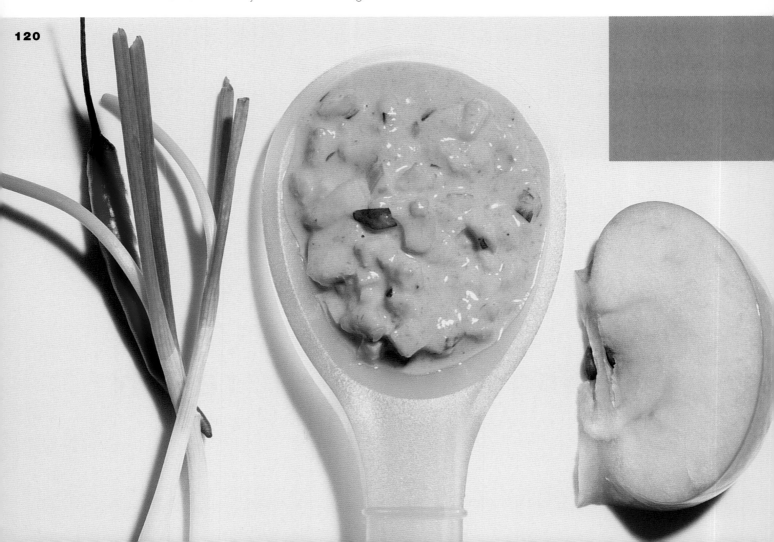

1 Fry the shallots gently in the butter, add the white wine, both types of vinegar, the sprig of thyme, salt and sprig of tarragon. **2** Cook, uncovered, until nearly all the liquid has evaporated. Discard the thyme and tarragon stalks, then gradually beat in the beurre noisette, adding a little at a time, so that the mixture thickens a little and becomes slightly creamy. **3** Just before serving, add the pepper and the chopped tarragon.

béarnaise relish

sauces

serves 4: 100 g finely chopped shallots   30 g butter   50 ml white wine
scant 1 tbsp sherry vinegar   1 tsp balsamic vinegar   sprig of thyme   salt
1 small sprig of tarragon   80 g butter, heated until golden brown (beurre noisette)
generous pinch of pepper   finely chopped leaves from a sprig of tarragon

serves 4: 5 shallots, sliced into thin rings   200 ml medium-dry sherry   200 ml double cream
1 tbsp Meaux mustard   1 tbsp traditional, coarse grain mustard

creamy mustard sauce

1 Sweat the shallots, then add the sherry and simmer, uncovered, until the liquid has reduced by half. Remove half the shallots and reserve. **2** Add the cream to the pan and simmer for 10 minutes. Beat in the mustard a little at a time without allowing the sauce to reach boiling point again. Purée until very smooth. **3** Just before serving, return the reserved shallots to the saucepan to give the sauce more body.

1 Slice the shallots very thinly. Remove the mushroom stalks and cut these and 2 of the caps into very small dice. **2** Reserve the other 2 caps for slicing into thin slivers just before serving the sauce, for garnish. **3** Fry the diced mushrooms in the oil, then transfer to a sieve to drain. **4** Fry the lardons in a heavy-bottomed saucepan until browned. Add the shallots, fry, then stir in the white wine. Simmer, uncovered, until all the liquid has evaporated. Add the concentrated stock and the drained diced mushrooms and simmer gently until the mushrooms are tender and the sauce has thickened somewhat. **5** Add the sherry vinegar, season to taste and serve, sprinkled with the raw slivers of mushroom.

mushroom compote

serves 4: 2 shallots   4 large fresh ceps   3 tbsp olive oil
50 g smoked streaky bacon, cut into lardons   200 ml dry white wine
200 ml white stock (page 126) boiled down to 100 ml (page 126)
1/2 tsp sherry vinegar   sea salt   pepper

serves 4: 30 g butter   30 g shallots, finely chopped   150 g button mushrooms
100 g shiitake mushrooms   125 ml dry white wine   250 ml white stock (page 126)
100 ml crème fraîche   1 sprig of tarragon   juice of 1 lemon
salt   pepper   90 g enoki mushrooms

white mushroom compote
sauces

1 Heat the butter in a wide, heavy-bottomed saucepan, add the shallots and fry without allowing to brown. **2** Add the button and shiitake mushrooms and fry, also without browning. Pour in the white wine and simmer, uncovered, until reduced by half. Then add the white stock, crème fraîche and tarragon. **3** Simmer, uncovered, until the liquid has reduced a little. Season with lemon juice, salt and pepper. Purée the sauce before serving garnished with the enoki mushrooms. **4** This sauce can be made with a wide variety of cultivated and wild mushrooms depending on availability and time of year.

123

1 Simmer the finely chopped shallots in the wine until reduced by two thirds. **2** Add the stock and boil for several minutes. Add the finely chopped chilli and a little pepper. **3** Just before serving, add the finely chopped gherkins, tongue, cooked shallots and tomato.

spicy shallot and
pickled tongue sauce
sauces

serves 4: 2 shallots   300 ml dry white wine
200 ml veal stock (page 126) reduced to a demi-glace   1 bird's eye chilli
pepper   3 gherkins   50 g pickled tongue, sliced and cut into short, thin matchstick strips
1 tbsp cooked shallots (see steps 1 and 2 of béarnaise relish on page 121)
1 tomato, skinned, deseeded, finely diced

serves 4: 100 g cockles or mussels, off the shell   60 g carpet shell clams, off the shell
6 smooth venus clams, red sections cut into thin strips   6 open smoked oysters, chopped
2 shallots   3 garlic cloves   200 ml dry white wine   1 sprig of thyme
100 ml strained liquor from the mussels, clams and oysters   250 ml double cream

shellfish sauce

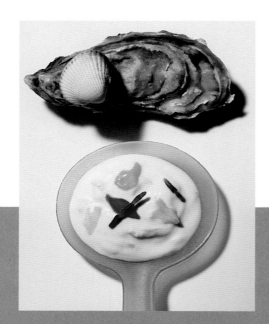

1 Have all the shellfish ready. Save as much liquor as possible when opening the cockles or mussels and strain through a sieve lined with a damp cloth. **2** Gently sweat the chopped shallots and garlic until tender. Add the white wine, thyme and shellfish liquor and simmer, uncovered, until reduced by half. Pour in the cream and simmer for another 10 minutes. Purée and strain through a conical sieve. **3** Add all the shellfish to this sauce. **4** Do not allow the sauce to boil after adding them; they should heat through but not cook.

1 Brown the pieces of beef well in a fairly deep, heavy-bottomed frying pan or a saucepan. **2** Add the honey, brown sugar, chilli, finely chopped ginger and galangal, mustard seeds, a pinch of white pepper and citrus juices, followed by the sherry vinegar and Dijon mustard, stirring and scraping the bottom of the pan. **3** Cook uncovered until the liquid has reduced by half, then add the veal stock. **4** Simmer gently for about 2 hours, then strain through a conical sieve. **5** To make the tomato mixture, sweat the onions gently in the olive oil then add the tomatoes, garlic, bouquet garni and pepper, cover and cook in a preheated oven at 160°C/gas mark 2 for 3 hours. **6** To make the shallots with vinegar, finely chop the shallots and sweat them in the butter. Add the wine vinegar and simmer until it has completely evaporated. **7** Stir into the concentrated stock along with the tomato mixture. Season if necessary.

barbecue sauce

serves 4: 250 g braising steak trimmings   1 tbsp honey   50 g brown cane sugar   1 bird's eye chilli
50 g fresh ginger   50 g galangal   1 tbsp mustard seeds   white pepper   100 ml lime juice
200 ml freshly pressed orange juice   100 ml sherry vinegar   1/2 tsp Dijon mustard
300 ml veal stock   **tomato mixture:** 1 onion   1 tbsp olive oil   300 g skinned, deseeded,
chopped tomatoes   2 garlic cloves, finely chopped   1 bouquet garni   1/2 tsp mignonette pepper
shallots with vinegar: 100 g shallots   30 g butter   100 ml red wine vinegar

court bouillon

2 carrots
1 onion
2 garlic cloves
200 ml dry white wine
sprig of thyme
1 bay leaf
salt
peppercorns

Cut the carrots and onion in half lengthwise. Partially crush the garlic cloves but leave them whole. Place all the ingredients in a large saucepan half-filled with water. Bring slowly to the boil. Use as required.

white stock

1 kg chicken carcasses
1 onion
1/2 leek, white part only
1 carrot
1/2 stick of celery
1 bay leaf
1 small sprig of thyme
3 sprigs of parsley
1/2 tsp white peppercorns
large pinch of sea salt

Break up the chicken carcasses so that they will fit comfortably in a fairly large stockpot or tall saucepan. Add 2 litres cold water and bring slowly to the boil, skimming off any scum that rises to the surface at repeated intervals. Add the vegetables, cut into fairly large pieces, herbs, peppercorns and the salt and simmer gently for at least 2 hours. Strain through a fine conical sieve.

veal stock

1 kg veal bones
1 onion
1/2 leek
1 carrot
2 tomatoes
1 tbsp tomato purée
1 tbsp plain flour
250 ml dry white wine
1 bouquet garni
1 tsp sea salt
1/2 tsp peppercorns
1 calf's foot

Oil a heavy roasting tin, add the chopped bones and roast in the oven at 200°C/gas mark 6 until browned. Set the bones aside. Add the vegetables, chopped into large dice, to the pan. Sweat until tender, stir in the tomato purée and flour and cook very gently for 10 minutes. Stir in the wine to dislodge the sediment. Transfer the contents of the tin to a stockpot, add the reserved veal bones, the bouquet garni, salt and peppercorns and enough water to cover the bones by 5 cm. Bring slowly to the boil, skimming off all the scum. Simmer very gently, uncovered, until the stock has reduced. Add the calf's foot and simmer gently for 24 hours.

concentrated chicken/duck stock

flesh from 2 free-range chicken legs
50 g chicken fat
1 onion, halved
3 garlic cloves
3 cm piece of fresh ginger
1 lemon grass bulb
1/2 tsp each ground mace, ground ginger and cardamom

flesh from 2 free-range duck legs
50g duck fat
1 onion, halved
3 garlic cloves
2 carrots, halved
1 bouquet garni

Chop chicken or duck flesh fairly coarsely and fry gently in the fat in a stock pot until pale golden brown. Add the remaining ingredients according to type of stock, and cover with cold water. Bring slowly to the boil and then simmer gently, removing the scum occasionally. Strain through a conical sieve, return to the pot and simmer to reduce by half.

a   s   i   c   s

groundnut oil
500 g braising veal, such as
flank, shoulder, knuckle, cut
into 5 cm cubes
75 g butter
1/2 head of garlic

Heat a little oil in a stockpot or
large saucepan, add the veal and
brown well all over.
Drain off all the oil and fat, add
the butter and heat while scraping
the browned deposits free from
the bottom of the pan with a
wooden spatula or spoon.
Add enough cold water to cover
the veal and simmer, uncovered
until nearly all the liquid has
evaporated and then add fresh
cold water to come half-way up
the veal. Repeat the reduction
until only a very small amount of
concentrated, dense liquid is left
in the pan (a jelly consistency
when cooled). Add water and
reduce three more times. Add
fresh, cold water yet again, this
time enough to cover the veal.
Add the garlic. Boil gently for
3 hours, then strain through a fine
conical sieve. The stock is now
ready for use.

fish stock

1 kg white fish bones and the
trimmings from the fish to be
served
1 onion
1 shallot
50 g button mushrooms
1 bouquet garni
large pinch of sea salt

Sweat the fish bones and
trimmings and the chopped
vegetables in a heavy-bottomed
saucepan or casserole. Pour in
just enough cold water to cover,
add the bouquet garni and salt
and bring to the boil. Skim the
scum from the surface. Adjust
the heat so the liquid gives only
an occasional bubble for
20 minutes. Strain through a
conical sieve, pressing firmly on
the contents to extract all the
juices. Leave to cool.

sauce américaine

2 shallots
1 carrot
3 tomatoes, skinned,
deseeded and very coarsely
chopped
100 g butter
20 ml whisky
100 ml dry white wine
2 lobster or crab shells
20 ml cognac
pinch of cayenne pepper

Fry the chopped shallots,
carrot and tomatoes gently for
2–3 minutes in a little of the
butter. Add the whisky,
followed by the wine and
simmer, uncovered to reduce
and then add 100 ml water.
Add the chopped lobster or
crab shells and simmer for
45 minutes. Stir in the
remaining butter, the cognac
and cayenne, then press
through a conical sieve.

rich beef sauce

1 kg braising steak, cut into
50 g cubes
100 ml groundnut oil
2 carrots
1 onion
6 garlic cloves
2 oranges
1 lemon
1 bouquet garni
1 tbsp mignonette pepper
1 litre dry red wine
500 ml veal stock
1/2 calf's foot

Brown the pieces of beef all
over in the oil in a stockpot.
Remove with a slotted spoon
and set aside. Sweat the diced
carrots and onion and the
crushed garlic in the oil left
behind. Return the meat to the
stockpot and add the quartered
oranges and lemon, the bouquet
garni, pepper, wine, veal stock
and calf's foot. Simmer for
2–3 hours, uncovered. Strain
and simmer to reduce further
if necessary.

4

fish

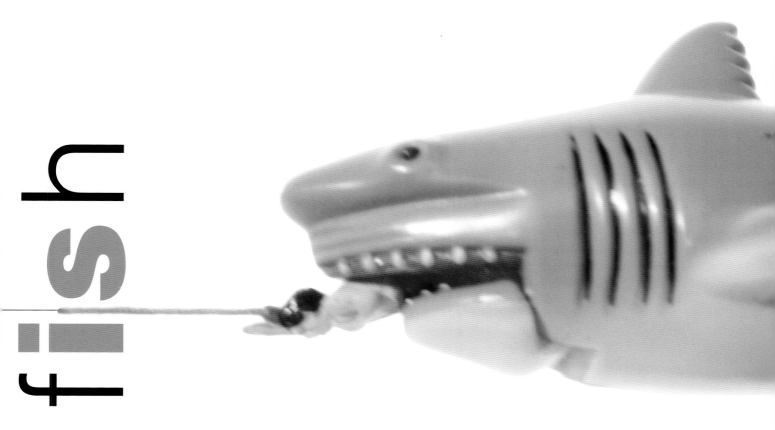

serves 4: 4 raw hen lobsters (females) weighing 500 g each   court bouillon (page 126)
100 ml white wine vinegar   1 carrot   1 celery stalk   1 onion   1 bouquet garni
200 ml lemon grass sauce (page 113)   8 fresh banana leaves
wines: United States: white   Santa Cruz Mountains   1997   Chardonnay
France: Alsace   white   1996   Riesling   Cuvée Frédéric Émile   F.E. Trimbach

fish lobsters baked
in banana leaves

1 Remove the lobster claws and cook them in court bouillon for 8 minutes. **2** Cook the lobster bodies for 3 minutes in a large stockpot of court bouillon with the vinegar, the coarsely sliced vegetables and the bouquet garni. **3** Leave to cool completely before cutting the lobsters in half lengthwise. Remove the coral and the tomalley (liver) and stir into the lemon grass sauce. Take care to remove the stomach sac from their bodies: it often contains sand. **4** Take the flesh from the claws, keeping it as intact as possible; reserve for the accompanying salad. Remove the flesh from the adjacent 'elbow' section of the claws and from the tail. Chop coarsely and add to the sauce. **5** Fill the body and tail cavities with the lemon grass sauce and lobster mixture. **6** Blanch the banana leaves in a large saucepan of boiling water, drain and refresh in iced water. **7** Place a banana leaf on the work surface, put another on top at right angles, forming a cross. Carefully bring the two halves of each lobster together and wrap up tightly in the banana leaves to form a parcel. **8** Tie securely with string and then grill or barbecue for 13 minutes. Remove the parcel from the heat and leave to stand for 2 minutes before serving.

130

lemon grass 113

▲ **sauce** ▼ **accompaniment**

green leaf, herb and plantain salad

2 very green plantains
oil for deep-frying
100 g wild rocket (riquette)
100 g baby spinach leaves
1/2 bunch of chervil
1/2 bunch of mint
2 sprigs of marjoram
2 sprigs of Thai basil
olive oil
salt
pepper
lobster claw meat
20 g butter

Peel the plantains and cut lengthwise into thin strips. Deep-fry in hot oil at 180°C for about 2 minutes. Drain on kitchen paper. Mix the salad and herbs, drizzle with olive oil and season. Add the plantains, and the lobster meat gently warmed through in the butter.

serves 4: thick wing of skate weighing 1.3 kg   1 litre court bouillon (page 126)
80 g cockles off the shell   50 g carpet shell clams off the shell
30 g red sections of smooth venus clams, cut into fine strips   120 ml dry white wine
wines: United States: white Santa Barbara County 1998 Viognier Jaffurs
France: Loire Valley white 1995 Vouvray Le Mont Huet

fish | poached skate

1 Place the skate in the court bouillon and heat gently to boiling point; poach gently for about 1 minute. Cook the shellfish in the wine as directed for youm koumg (page 40). **2** Trim the skin of the skate and use a sharp cook's fish knife to take the skate carefully off the cartilaginous bone, keeping it in 2 pieces. Cut these in half. **3** Re-assemble the skate pieces in a wide steamer and steam until nearly done. Garnish with the shellfish and steam briefly to reheat the shellfish.

▲ **sauce**   ▼ **accompaniment**

buttered baby spinach

500 g baby spinach leaves
50 g butter
1 garlic clove
salt
pepper

Remove the spinach stalks. Heat the butter in a frying pan until it turns golden brown. Sprinkle in the spinach leaves and stir during their brief cooking with the garlic speared on to a fork. Season with salt and pepper.

serves 4: 1 Dover sole weighing 1.5 kg   100 g caster sugar   dash of balsamic vinegar
200 ml spicy tomato syrup (page 115)   20 g garlic, chopped
10 g fresh ginger, chopped   1 tbsp olive oil
wines: United States: white Napa Valley 1998 Chardonnay Miura
France: Burgundy white Côtes-de-Beaune 1998 Puligny-Montrachet J.-M. Boillot

grilled lacquered sole

fish

1 Carefully trim off the outside edge of the fish, remove the skin from both sides and cut off the head and fins. Use strong kitchen scissors to cut along the backbone, dividing it lengthwise in half; cut these in half. **2** Heat the sugar and 2 tablespoons water together until caramelised. Remove from the heat, add the balsamic vinegar, then simmer until reduced by half. **3** Stir in the tomato syrup, add the garlic, ginger and olive oil and simmer, uncovered, until reduced to a glossy sauce, like a lacquer. Strain through a conical sieve. **4** Brush the pieces of sole liberally with the lacquer and roast in a preheated oven at 200°C/gas mark 6 for 8–10 minutes, brushing with the remaining lacquer half-way through.

135

spicy tomato coulis
68

▲ **sauce**   ▼ **accompaniment**

baby leeks with sesame seed coating

12 very thin baby leeks
3 eggs
1 tbsp oil
pinch salt
pinch pepper
100 g white sesame seeds

Cut the white parts of the leeks into 7 cm lengths. Add to a large saucepan of boiling salted water, then simmer very gently for 5 minutes. Drain, refresh in iced water then drain well. Beat the eggs, oil, salt and pepper together. Dip the leeks in the egg mixture, then roll in the sesame seeds. Fry in oil until the sesame coating is golden brown.

serves 4: 1 very large John Dory   2–3 tbsp olive oil   juice of 2 limes   salt   pepper
wines: Luxemburg: white Stadtbredimus-Luxembourg 1997
Riesling Grand Premier Cru Cep d'Or
France: Loire Valley 1996 Pouilly-Fumé Cuvée Majorum Michel Redde

fish grilled john dory fillets

1 Take the flesh off the fish in 4 neat fillets; if they are very thick, cut them open from the thicker side towards the outer edge without cutting through, and open out, like a book. Lay in a single layer in a grill pan, sprinkle with the olive oil, lime juice, and season with salt and pepper. **2** Preheat the grill until very hot. Grill the fish quickly until just done to avoid drying out the fillets. **3** Remove from the grill and spoon the cooking juices over the fillets.

136 ◄ creamy mustard 122

▲ **sauce**   ▼ **accompaniment**

warm/hot spring vegetables

50 g very thin French beans
4 baby leeks
4 very fresh baby carrots
4 baby courgettes
4 slim asparagus spears
8 spring onions
2 tbsp olive oil
juice of 1/2 lemon

Steam the whole beans and leeks. Use a mandolin to cut the carrots, courgettes and asparagus into slivers. Chop the spring onions.Stir-fry all the vegetables in the oil in a wok until tender but still crisp, sprinkling with lemon juice.

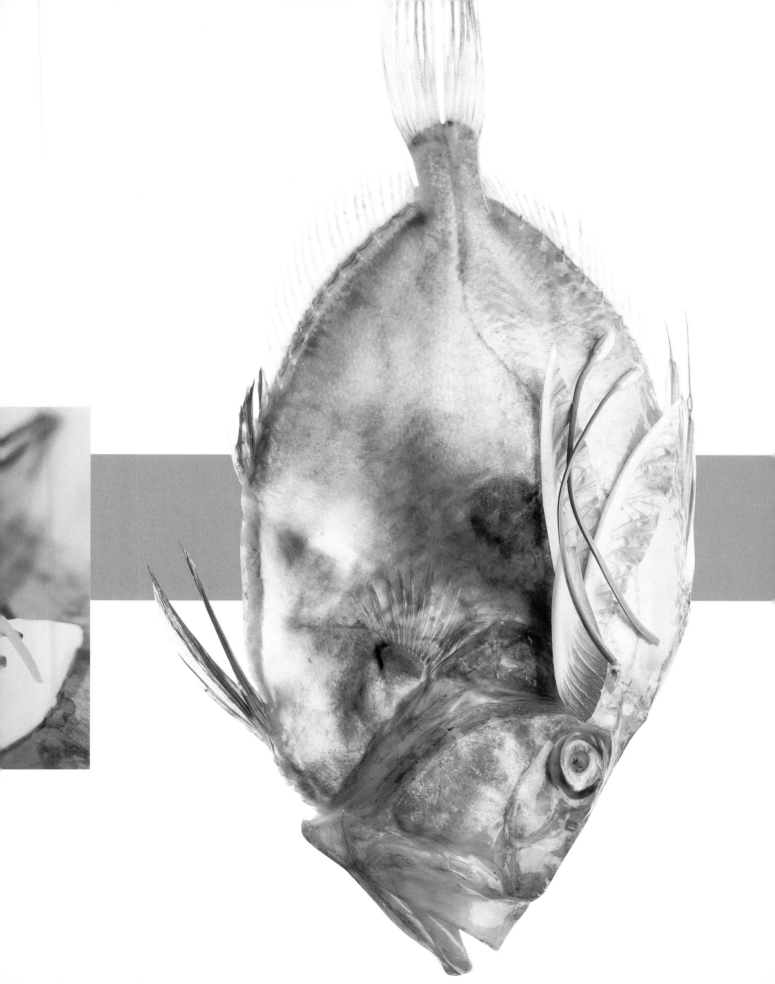

sauce ▲ béarnaise 121

1 The salmon fillets should measure about 10 x 5 cm.
Sprinkle with salt and pepper. **2** Heat a very little oil in
a heatproof casserole and brown the fish lightly on
both sides. **3** Transfer to a preheated oven at 200°C/gas
mark 6 and roast for about 5 minutes. Take care not to
overcook the salmon otherwise it will become dry.

fish **roast salmon**

serves 4:   4 thick, mid-cut fillets of skinned wild Scotish salmon each weighing 180 g
salt   pepper   olive oil
wines: Spain: red Sardon de Duero 1996 Abadia Retuerta Finca Abadia Retuerta
France: Languedoc red 1998 Saint-Chinian Le Travers de Marceau Domaine Rimbert

1 baking potato
2 eggs
125 g fine fry breadcrumbs
4 young purple artichokes
100 g wild rocket (riquette)
CHOUX PASTRY:
30 g butter
pinch of salt
pinch of caster sugar
40 g plain flour, sifted
1 large egg
salt
pepper

accompaniment ▼

potato fingers with artichoke hearts

Bake the potato until very tender.
Scoop out the flesh and pass through a
ricer or fine sieve.
To make a choux pastry, bring 250 ml
water to the boil with the butter, salt
and sugar in a heavy-bottomed
saucepan. Remove from the heat, add
all the flour at once and beat quickly
using a balloon whisk. Place over a
fairly high heat and continue to beat
until the mixture leaves the sides and
base of the pan cleanly. Remove from
the heat and thoroughly beat in the egg.
Mix with the potato and add a little salt
and pepper.
Using a piping bag fitted with a 1 cm
plain nozzle, pipe 12 cm lengths on a
baking sheet. Put in the freezer for
5 minutes while you lightly beat the
remaining 2 eggs and spread out the
breadcrumbs on a plate.
Dip the potato fingers in the egg, then
coat with the breadcrumbs.Deep-fry at
180°C until puffed and golden brown.
Meanwhile, prepare the artichokes and
cut them into slivers. Arrange the
artichokes and wild rocket in bowls and
stand the potato fingers among them.

serves 4: 1 very fresh fillet of red tuna   50 g satay spices   salt   pepper   olive oil
wines: Portugal: red Alentejo 1994 Quinta do Carmo Quinta Estremoz
France: Côtes-du-Rhône 1997 Châteauneuf-du-Pape Les Bartavelles Colombo

fish tuna à la plancha

1 Cut the tuna fillet into cylinders 5 cm in diameter and 12 cm long. **2** Marinate in the satay spices for 2 hours. **3** Season the tuna fillets with salt and pepper, heat the oil in a frying pan and then sear the tuna evenly; they should be rare inside. **4** Serve sliced with your choice of accompaniment and sprinkled with salt and pepper.

140

▼ **accompaniment**

stir-fried mixed vegetables

2 small courgettes
1/4 cauliflower
2 young, very fresh carrots
4 young artichokes, preferably purple
100 g shiitake mushrooms
2 small yellow courgettes
100 g flat green beans
1–1 1/2 tbsp olive oil
2 tbsp soy sauce
salt
8 garlic chives, roughly chopped
8 garlic cloves, sliced
12 Thai spring onions
16 small Cos lettuce leaves
50 g green leaf part of Swiss chard, or spinach

Thinly slice the vegetables using a mandolin. Heat the oil in a wok and briefly stir-fry the vegetables over a high heat. Sprinkle with the soy sauce and a little salt. Add the garlic chives, garlic and spring onions, followed by the leaf vegetables, stir and serve.

serves 4: 250 ml coconut milk   juice of 1 lemon   2 tbsp olive oil   salt   pepper
4 pieces of thick, very fresh cod fillet, weighing 180 g each
wines: Italy: white Piedmont 1997 Chardonnay Gaja & Rey Gaja
France: Burgundy white Côtes-de-Beaune 1997 Puligny-Montrachet J.-M. Boillot

fish cod with coconut milk

1 Mix the coconut milk with the lemon juice, olive oil and seasoning. Add the cod and leave to marinate in a cool place for 1 hour. Drain the coconut milk into a saucepan and boil gently, uncovered, for 15–20 minutes to reduce and thicken. **2** Bake the cod in a preheated oven at 180°C/gas mark 4 for about 4 minutes. **3** Pour a thin coating of coconut sauce over each serving of cod.

142

lemon relish
107

▲ **sauce**   ▼ **accompaniment**

swiss chard with tomatoes

bunch of Swiss chard
1 tbsp plain flour
juice of 1 lemon
5 tomatoes
olive oil
10 g butter
500 ml white stock (page 126)
salt
pepper
1 garlic clove

Cut the green leaves from the chard stalks. Peel off the outer layer from the stalks. Put the flour into a saucepan and stir in plenty of cold water, add the lemon juice and chard stalks and boil until very tender. Drain and cut into lozenge-shaped pieces. Peel and quarter the tomatoes and remove the seeds. Heat a little oil in a sauté pan, add the tomatoes, then the chard. Stir in the butter, stock and seasoning. Blanch the chard leaves briefly and add them with the garlic to the chard stalks and tomatoes. Serve.

curry 120

▲ **sauce** ▼ **accompaniment**

thai rice

250 g Thai jasmine rice
1 egg
2 spring onions, finely
chopped
dash of soy sauce
2 garlic chives, chopped

Cook the rice, preferably
in a rice steamer, until
tender but not at all
sticky. Break the egg
into an oiled wok and
beat while adding the
spring onions, soy
sauce and garlic chives.
Add the rice and stir-fry
for 2 minutes.

serves 4: 1.25 kg squid   2 tbsp olive oil
2 spring onions   4 tbsp coconut milk
1 tbsp garlic chilli sauce
50 g white sesame seeds
marinade: juice of 1/2 lemon   100 ml olive oil
wines: New Zealand: white Nelson 1998
Sauvignon blanc Neudorf
France: Côtes-du-Rhône white 1999
Condrieu Les Chaillets Cuilleron

marinated and seared squid with quick-braised tentacles

fish

1 Cut the squid body into quarters. Score the flesh at 5 cm intervals, to make a lattice pattern; this will prevent the squid distorting as it cooks. **2** Mix the marinade ingredients together, add the squid pieces and turn to coat. **3** Blanch the 8 tentacles and peel off the skin. Thinly slice the tentacles and fry over a high heat in the oil with the chopped spring onions. Add the coconut milk and the garlic chilli sauce. **4** Drain the squid from the marinade and cover the scored side with sesame seeds. Fry briefly with the seeded side downwards over a high heat to lightly brown the seeds and allow them to release their flavour without cooking the squid too much. **5** Cut the squid pieces into thin slivers before serving with the tentacle mixture and a bowl of the sauce.

serves 4: 1 gilt-head bream weighing 2 kg   2 tbsp groundnut oil   30 g butter
topping: 1 egg   200 ml single cream   30 g finely chopped onions, cooked and cooled
leaves from 1 sprig of tarragon, coarsely chopped   2 garlic cloves
150 g raw prawns, peeled   12 raw tiger prawns, peeled   groundnut oil   15 g butter
wines: Germany: white Moselle 1997 Riesling Aulese Trocken Brauneberger-Juffer Fritz Haag
France: Bourgogne white Côtes-de-Beaune 1998 Meursault Le Limozin M. Bouzereau

bream fish

with double prawn topping

1 Carefully remove the flesh from the bream in 4 fillets, then remove the skin and trim the fillets into 4 rectangular shapes. Keep the head, tail and 100 g trimmings for the topping. **2** To make the topping, pound these trimmings to a paste, add the egg and cream and mix well. Add the onions, tarragon, crushed garlic and chopped small prawns. **3** Cover one side of each fillet at room temperature with this mixture and press the tiger prawns firmly into it. Place very carefully, topping side down, in a wide frying pan containing a little hot groundnut oil and butter and cook until the topping is just set and the prawn cooked. **4** Carefully turn the fish so that the topping is uppermost and cook until the fish is done.

mushroom compote
122

▲ **sauce**   ▼ **accompaniment**

mushroom, spinach and walnut salad

4 small, closed-cap ceps
olive oil
juice of 1 lemon
salt
pepper
400 g baby spinach leaves
100 g fresh walnuts

Rinse the ceps and cut into thin slivers using a mandolin, then toss in a little olive oil, half the lemon juice, salt and pepper.
Discard the spinach stalks and toss the leaves with the mushrooms. Remove the thin skin from the walnuts and add to the mushrooms and spinach.

serves 4: 8 oranges   40 g Szechuan peppercorns   2 tbsp olive oil   juice of 2 lemons   salt   pepper
4 rock (spiny) lobsters, weighing 500 g each   court bouillon   12 small bok choi
chutney: 8 green mangoes   1 tbsp tamarind paste   1 tbsp chopped chilli   10 g mint leaves
10 g coriander leaves   3 garlic cloves   2 tbsp balsamic vinegar   salt
wines: United States: white Santa Barbara County 1996 Chardonnay
Nuits Blanches Au Bon Climat
France: Champagne 1990 Dom Perignon Moët & Chandon

fish

spiny lobster, cape style

148

1 To make the chutney, peel the mangoes and cut all the flesh into fairly small pieces. Process with the tamarind paste, chopped chilli, mint, coriander, garlic and vinegar to obtain a very thick purée. Add salt if necessary and chill until required. **2** Use a canelle knife to remove the zest from the oranges. Spread the strips out on a baking sheet with the Szechuan peppercorns and put in the bottom of an oven heated to its lowest setting for about 3 hours to dry. Then pound to a powder with a pestle and mortar and whisk with the olive oil, lemon juice, salt and pepper to make the vinaigrette. Set aside. **3** Cook the spiny lobsters in court bouillon for 6 minutes. Leave to cool before taking all the white flesh from the tails. **4** Cook the bok choi in boiling salted water. Drain and refresh in iced water and slice in half. **5** Cut the lobster tails into thick, slanting slices and place in the middle of a bamboo steamer compartment. **6** Arrange the halved bok choi around them; trickle the vinaigrette over the steamer contents. Steam to warm through. Serve accompanied by the mango chutney.

serves 4: 8 red mullet weighing 120 g each   1 litre oil for deep-frying   1 tbsp olive oil
tempura batter: 200 g plain flour   20 g instant dried yeast   5 g ground Espelette chillies
salt   pepper   500 ml water   4 basil leaves   **tempura vegetables:** 1 aubergine   1 courgette
1 fennel bulb   green parts of 12 garlic chives   green parts of 12 spring onions
4 courgette flowers   8 asparagus spears   **curry sauce:** 50 ml olive oil   1 tbsp curry paste
80 g squid   1/2 green apple   400 ml coconut milk   salt   pepper
wines: New Zealand: white Marlborough 1999 Sauvignon blanc Cloudy Bay
France: Côtes-du-Rhône white 1999 Condrieu Les Chaillets Cuilleron

fish seared red mullet

150

1 To make the tempura batter, mix the flour, yeast, chilli pepper, salt and pepper and gradually work in enough water to make a coating batter. Set aside until frothy **2** Remove the scales from the red mullets. Trim, gut and fillet the fish. Refrigerate until needed. **3** To prepare the tempura vegetables, thinly slice the aubergine and courgette lengthwise using a mandolin. Halve the fennel and slice lengthwise with the mandolin. Snip the garlic chives and spring onion leaves into 7 cm lengths; snip the courgette flowers in half lengthwise. **4** To make the curry sauce, stir the olive oil and curry paste together in a small saucepan over a moderate heat for a few minutes. Finely dice the squid and the apple, add to the pan, reduce the heat to very low and cook for a few minutes more. Stir in the coconut milk. **5** Cook, uncovered, over a moderate heat until the liquid has reduced to a coating consistency. Strain through a conical sieve and reserve the apple and squid dice left in the sieve. Purée the sauce then return the apple and squid. Add salt and pepper and keep hot in the top of a double boiler. **6** Half-fill a deep-fryer with oil and heat to 180°C. Dip the vegetables and flowers in turn in the batter. Gently shake off the excess and deep-fry until pale golden brown. Transfer to kitchen paper to drain. **7** Fry the red mullet fillets, skin side down, in a very little olive oil in a hot frying pan. When the skin is fairly crisp turn the fish and cook until only just done. **8** Arrange the tempura selection and the mullet fillets on a heated large plate, spoon over a little curry sauce and garnish with a sprinkling of chopped basil leaves.

5

meat &

poultry

serves 8: binding mixture: 100 g very finely minced breast of veal   1 egg   100 ml single cream
salt   pepper   **veal burgers:** 70 g onions in 5 mm dice   1 tbsp olive oil
400 g lean veal, cut into 5 mm dice   300 g breast of veal, finely chopped   1 garlic clove, finely chopped
leaves from 2 sprigs of tarragon   1/2 tsp finely chopped chervil   1 tbsp finely chopped parsley   salt   pepper
straw potato cakes: 500 g waxy potatoes, such as Charlotte or Ratte   30 ml oil   30 g butter
garnish: 2 large white onions   8 slices streaky bacon or pancetta
wines: Australia: red McLaren Vale – Coonawarra 1996 Cabernet Sauvignon The Angelus
Wirra Wirra   **France:** Bordeaux red Pessac-Leognan 1996 Château Brown

veal burgers with straw potato cakes

meat

154

gherkin and onion 116
barbecue 124
sauce ▲

1 First combine the binding mixture ingredients. **2** To make the burgers, sweat the onions in the olive oil and leave to cool. **3** Stir the lean veal and the veal breast into the binding mixture. Add the cold onions, garlic, coarsely chopped or snipped tarragon, the chervil, parsley, salt and pepper. **4** Shape into 8 burgers. Heat a heavy, non-stick frying pan, add the burgers and cook for 4 minutes on each side without browning too darkly. Keep warm. **5** To make the straw potato cakes, coarsely grate the potatoes into very fine, short strips. Blot well with kitchen paper. Heat the hot oil and butter in a very small, non-stick frying pan, add about one-eighth of the potatoes, pressing down well and spreading out in a fairly thin, even layer to form a potato cake. Cook for 2 minutes on each side, turning carefully until golden brown. Repeat to make 8 cakes. Transfer to kitchen paper to drain. **6** To make the garnish, slice the onions into fine rings. Fry over a moderate heat until pale golden brown. Drain on kitchen paper. **7** Place the bacon or pancetta slices on a baking sheet, cover with another baking sheet and cook in a preheated oven at 150°C/gas mark 1 1/2 until lightly browned. Alternatively, dry-fry the bacon in a non-stick frying pan. **8** Place a potato cake on each heated plate, add some fried onion rings followed by a burger. Top with 2 crisp bacon slices, a few more onions and, finally, another potato cake.

accompaniment ▲ lettuce hearts

serves 8: 4 large poussins, weighing 500–600 g each   1 tbsp olive oil
1/2 tsp ground Espelette chilli peppers   juice of 2 lemons   3 tbsp smooth Dijon mustard
3 tbsp Meaux mustard   1 tbsp double cream   salt   pepper
wines: United States: red Carneros 1996 Pinot Meunier Domaine Chandon
France: Burgundy red Côte Chalonnaise 1997 Mercurey Château de Chamirey

poultry

grilled spatchcocked poussins, american style

1 Cut the poussins' skin open along the backbone with poultry shears and carefully cut out the backbone and ribs, working the skin and flesh away from them neatly. Make an incision at the base of each thigh, underneath, where it joins the body and tuck the end of the drumstick into it. This is known as 'à la crapaudine'. Or, simply cut the birds along the breast bones, open them out flat, using the backbone as the 'hinge'. **2** Marinate the birds in a cool place in the oil, chilli and lemon juice. **3** Mix the two mustards with the cream and smear over the birds. Season. **4** Barbecue or roast in a preheated oven at 220°C/gas mark 7 for 20–30 minutes until the juices run clear. Serve with your choice of sauce and accompaniment.

spicy shallot & pickled tongue 123

▲ **sauce**

▼ **accompaniment**

stuffed tomatoes and potato straws

4 large, ripe vine tomatoes
salt
pepper
slow-baked tomato quarters (step 2, page 80)
thyme
vegetable oil
600 g potatoes

Cut off the tops off the tomatoes as 'lids'. Scoop out the seeds and season inside with salt and pepper. Fill with slow-baked tomatoes and place in a baking dish. Sprinkle with thyme and a little olive oil and cover with foil. Bake in a preheated oven at 140°C/gas mark 1 for 1 1/2 hours. Cut the potatoes into long, thin strips, put in a large bowl of cold water, then drain and blot thoroughly dry in a large, clean cloth. Fry in a deep-fryer at 160°C for a few minutes until lightly coloured. Drain on kitchen paper. Just before serving, deep-fry the potatoes in oil preheated to 200°C until golden brown. Drain and sprinkle with salt to taste.

serves 8: knob of butter   2 tbsp oil   800 g boned and rolled rib of Scotish beef, untied, cut into 4 lengthwise then across the centre and each piece re-rolled and tied securely, to make 8 mini-roasts   salt   pepper   **beef compote:** 500 g braising steak, cut into 8 cm cubes   1 onion   1 carrot   3 shallots   6 chopped garlic cloves   1 tbsp plain flour, dry-cooked until brown   500 ml red wine   1/2 orange, halved   juice of 2 oranges   juice of 1 lemon   250 ml veal stock (page 126)   bouquet garni   10 slow-baked tomato segments or 'petals' (step 2, page 80)   3 tbsp stoned black olives   100 g small white pickled onions in wine vinegar   salt   pepper

wines: Australia: red Barossa Valley 1997 Shiraz-Cabernet Sauvignon Bin 389 Penfolds
France: Bordeaux red Pomerol 1995 Château Bonalgue

rare breed beef mini-roasts
beef compote with
tomatoes and olives

meat

sauce   ▶ rich beef 127   ▼ accompaniment

pumpkin commas

2 pumpkin slices
olive oil
generous pinch of salt
generous pinch of mignonette pepper

Cut the peeled pumpkin slices into comma shapes, 3 cm thick. Fry in the oil until lightly browned, then season with salt and pepper.

1 To make the beef compote, brown the braising steak well in a little oil and butter in a heavy, flameproof casserole. Season and set aside. **2** Add the finely diced onion, carrot and shallots, and the garlic to the casserole and fry until lightly browned. Return the browned beef to the casserole, sprinkle with the cooked flour and stir for a couple of minutes. **3** Stir in the wine, orange quarters and citrus juices. Simmer, uncovered, to reduce by a quarter then pour in the stock and the bouquet garni. Cook gently for 2–3 hours, until the meat can be easily broken up with a fork. **4** Drain off the liquid and reserve. Tease the pieces of meat into fibres using two forks; discard any fat, gristle or skin. Keep warm in the oven. **5** Strain the liquid through a conical sieve and reduce further if necessary to make a rich gravy. **6** Mix the shredded meat with the gravy for a consistency that is moist but not sloppy; add the slow-baked tomato 'petals', the halved black olives and strained pickled onions. Add salt and pepper to taste. **7** Heat the butter and oil in a large flameproof casserole. Add the mini-roasts in batches and cook each for 2 minutes until well browned. Season with salt and pepper before transferring to a preheated oven at 220°C/gas mark 7 to roast for 5 minutes. **8** Time the cooking so the meat can 'rest' for 5 minutes before being served with the beef compote.

serves 4: 200 ml olive oil   24 small fillets from free-range chickens
salt   pepper   dash of soy sauce
wines: Chile: red 1997 Merlot Clos Apalta
France: Loire Valley white 1995 Vouvray Le Mont Huet

poultry

seared
chicken fillets

1 Heat the oil and lightly fry the chicken for 4 minutes, turning occasionally, until it is lightly browned and cooked through. **2** Season with salt, pepper and soy sauce. Serve with your choice of sauce and accompaniment.

ginger and herb 109
tandoori 113

sauce ▲   **accompaniment** ▼

stir-fried vegetables mikado

3 yellow courgettes
3 green courgettes
4 carrots
1 black radish
8 Thai spring onions
100 g enoki mushrooms
1 tbsp olive oil
salt
pepper
2 tbsp light soy sauce

Cut all the vegetables into strips 15 cm long and 5 mm thick. Stir-fry in a wok with a little olive oil. Season with salt and pepper and add a sprinkling of soy sauce in the last moments of stir-frying.

serves 4: 24 boned chicken wings from fresh, free-range, corn-fed birds
80 g chicken meat   **tandoori marinade:** 10 g mature Cheddar or blue cheese
100 ml plain yogurt   100 ml crème fraîche   20 g finely chopped fresh ginger
7 g finely chopped garlic   pinch of ground mace   pinch of ground cardamom seeds
1/2 bunch of coriander leaves, finely chopped   2 bird's eye chillies

poultry tandoori chicken wings

1 Make the marinade at least 4 hours but not more than 2 days in advance. Mix all the ingredients and marinate the chicken wings overnight. **2** To make the stuffing, process all the ingredients to a paste in a food processor. Spoon into a piping bag fitted with a fairly small plain nozzle. **3** Remove the chicken wings from the marinade. Pipe a small amount of stuffing into each one. Put in a roasting tin and spread with the marinade. **4** Roast in a preheated oven at 250°C/gas mark 9 for about 15 minutes.

160

tandoori 113

▲ **sauce**   ▼ **accompaniment**

noodle and asparagus moulds

12 spring onions, finely chopped
olive oil
80 g diced, cooked breast of veal
200 g pre-soaked Chinese rice noodles
100 g fresh Chinese black mushrooms
100 g shiitake mushrooms
8 green asparagus spears
1 tbsp light soy sauce
500 ml single cream
3 eggs
10 g finely chopped coriander
salt
pepper

Fry the spring onions in a little oil with the veal, noodles, mushrooms, asparagus tips and finely chopped upper stalks. Sprinkle with soy sauce and leave to cool. Stir in the cream, eggs, coriander and seasoning. Transfer to 4 ramekins 12 cm in diameter and 5 cm deep. Cook in a bain-marie in a preheated oven at 180°C/gas mark 4 for 20 minutes. Remove from the bain-marie and leave until cold. Unmould and reheat and brown in a little oil in a large frying pan.

stuffing: 80 g minced or finely chopped chicken   40 g slow-cooked chopped onions
pinch of very finely chopped garlic   50 g shiitake mushrooms, fried then finely chopped
20 g Chinese vermicelli, cooked and chopped   1 tbsp flat leaf parsley
1 tbsp finely chopped coriander leaves
wines: Chile: red Requinoa 1998 Cabernet Sauvignon Vieilles Vignes Château Los Boldos
France: Jura white 1996 L'Étoile-en Mont Genezet Voorhuis-Henquet

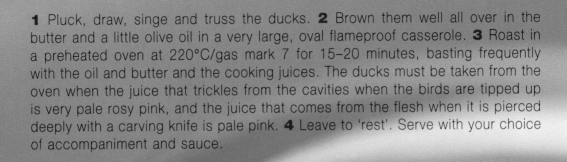

1 Pluck, draw, singe and truss the ducks. **2** Brown them well all over in the butter and a little olive oil in a very large, oval flameproof casserole. **3** Roast in a preheated oven at 220°C/gas mark 7 for 15–20 minutes, basting frequently with the oil and butter and the cooking juices. The ducks must be taken from the oven when the juice that trickles from the cavities when the birds are tipped up is very pale rosy pink, and the juice that comes from the flesh when it is pierced deeply with a carving knife is pale pink. **4** Leave to 'rest'. Serve with your choice of accompaniment and sauce.

sauce ▲ bigarade 118

▼ **accompaniment**

noodles with spring onions and mushrooms

200 g egg noodles
12 spring onions
100 g cooked duck, in thin strips
12 garlic chive stalks
70 g shiitake mushrooms
100 ml duck stock (page 126)

Add the noodles to a saucepan of boiling salted water; remove when only just tender. Stir-fry the chopped spring onions with the duck, chopped garlic chives and shiitake mushrooms. Add the duck stock and cook briefly, stirring and turning, then add the noodles, toss and serve.

serves 4: 2 undressed free-range ducks, such as Gressingham, weighing 1.25–1.5 kg each
30 g butter   2 tbsp olive oil
wines: United States: red California 1996 Zinfandel Lytin Springs Ridge
France: Burgundy red Côtes-de-Beaune 1997 Santenay La Maladière Girardin

roast duck

poultry

163

serves 4: 4 sets of 4 pork ribs, about 10 x 15 cm   1 litre white stock (page 126)
150 g unsalted roasted peanuts   **marinade:** 50 g ginger, finely chopped
20 g garlic cloves, finely chopped   2 lemon grass bulbs   5 cardamom pods, crushed
5 tbsp dark soy sauce   10 tbsp honey   5 tbsp sweet/acid tomato sauce (page 112)
500 ml white stock (page 126)

meat [acquered pork spare ribs

1 To make the marinade, combine the ingredients and cook
for 15 minutes. Leave to cool then pour over the spare ribs of
pork and marinate in a cool place overnight. **2** Drain off and
reserve the marinade. Brown the ribs in a large flameproof
casserole with the flavourings. **3** Add the white stock and place
in a preheated oven at 160°C/gas mark 3 for 2–3 hours.
4 Remove the sets of ribs from the casserole, divide into ribs
and set aside. Strain the cooking liquid through a conical sieve.
Reduce by boiling uncovered on the hob and then mix with the
marinade. Continue to cook until reduced to a thick, syrupy
sauce. **5** Coat the spare ribs liberally in the sauce and peanuts
and roast them in a preheated oven at 200°C/gas mark 6 for
10–15 minutes until very tender and crisp.

164

peanut 117

sauce ▲ **accompaniment ▼**

pommes à la maxim's

4 large waxy
potatoes
25 g clarified butter
salt
pepper

Cut the potatoes lengthwise
into 3 mm slices, using a
mandolin. Overlap them in
a single layer in a roasting
tin or shallow baking dish
and brush with the clarified
butter. Season with salt and
pepper and bake in a
preheated oven at 160°C/
gas mark 2 for 1 1/2 hours.

flavourings: 1 garlic clove   large piece of fresh ginger   1 lemon grass bulb, finely chopped
5 cardamom pods   large pinch of sea salt   fine salt   pepper
wines: Spain: red Priorat 1996 Clos Mogador René Barbier
France: Côtes-du-Rhône red 1996 Hermitage Sorrel

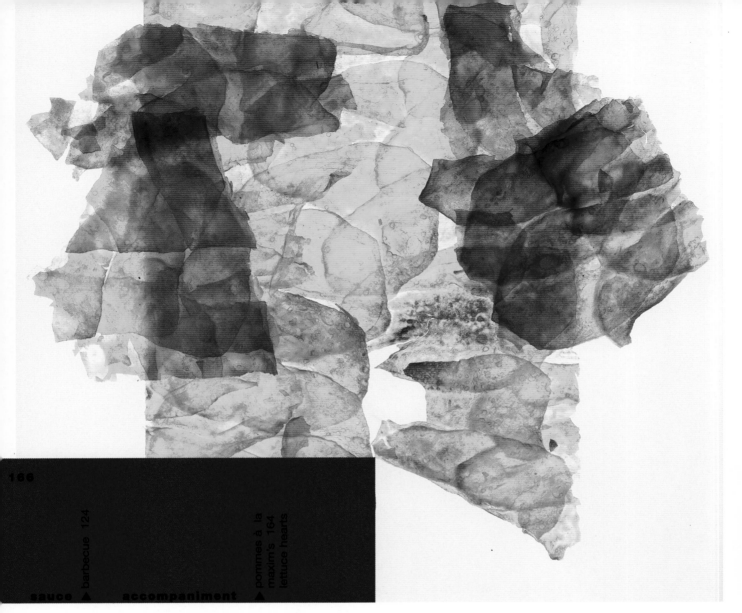

sauce ▲ barbecue 124

accompaniment ▲ pommes à la maxim's 164 lettuce hearts

1 To make the marinade, heat the ingredients together very gently for 10 minutes.
2 Brush liberally over the beef fillets. **3** Leave to marinate overnight. **4** Brush the beef liberally with marinade again just before roasting in a preheated oven at 250°C/gas mark 9 for 8–10 minutes. The beef should be well-browned on the outside and very rare inside, otherwise it will be dry.

meat ⎣fill⎦et of beef

serves 8: 2 fillets of rare breed beef, weighing 800 g each   salt   pepper
marinade: 20 g finely chopped fresh ginger   30 g garlic   3 lemon grass bulbs, finely chopped
10 cardamom pods, lightly crushed   5 tbsp dark soy sauce   5 tbsp honey
3 tbsp tomato ketchup   3 bird's eye chillies   juice of 1 lime   juice of 1 orange
wines: Australia: red Barossa Velley 1996 Shiraz E & E Black Pepper
France: Bordeaux red Pessac-Leognan 1994 La Chapelle de la Mission
(Second wine of Château La Mission Haut Brion)

In France, boeuf de Coutancie 'Perigord Vert' is used. This comes from 5-year-old, grass-fed Limousin cows that have never calved. They are 'finished' indoors for 4–5 months on a 70 per cent cereal 30 percent grass diet and given 2–3 litres of beer to drink daily. The cows are also massaged twice a day. This regime yields very tender, well-flavoured beef. The nearest equivalent is well-hung beef from a rare breed.

1 Remove the zest from the lemons and dry in a low oven. Chop finely. **2** Season the chicken suprêmes with pepper and salt. **3** Sear in a very hot, lightly oiled heavy frying pan, turning frequently until they are cooked through and well browned but still juicy. **4** Carve each suprême into slanting slices, re-assemble on heated plates and sprinkle with the lemon zests.

poultry

seared chicken suprêmes

serves 4: 2 unwaxed lemons   4 suprêmes (breast and first section of wing) of fresh, free-range, corn-fed chickens   salt   pepper

1 Heat the oil and butter in a large frying pan until very hot. Add the steaks and fry for 1–3 minutes on each side, depending on the thickness and how rare you like them. **2** Sprinkle with a little salt and pepper and serve.

pan-fried entrecôte steak
meat

serves 8: 2 tbsp oil   30 g butter   4 thick, entrecôte steaks from rare breed beef
salt   pepper

serves 4–6: 1 carrot   1 onion   4 garlic cloves   300 g rolled breast of veal
1 bouquet garni   500 ml white stock (page 126)   600 g boned rump end of loin of veal
wines: United States: red Napa Valley 1996 Cabernet-Sauvignon Staglin Family Vineyards
France: Champagne Billecart-Salmon Rosé

braised and roast veal

meat

1 Finely dice the carrot and onion, and crush the garlic cloves with the flat of a large knife but leave whole. **2** Brown the breast of veal lightly in a pan with the carrot, onion, garlic and bouquet garni. Add the white stock and simmer very gently for 3 hours, until the veal is very tender. Leave to cool before carving into 4 thick slices. Brown the slices over a high heat in a large frying pan, allowing 3 minutes per side. **3** Spit-roast or roast the veal loin in a preheated oven at 220°C/gas mark 7 for about 20 minutes, basting occasionally. **4** Carve the roast veal and put 2 slices on each heated plate with a slice of browned veal breast.

sauce ▲ rich veal stock 127   **accompaniment ▼**   171

coarsely mashed carrots

250 g organic carrots
3 tbsp olive oil
pinch of ground cumin
salt

Boil the carrots for
7 minutes in a large
saucepan of salted
water. Drain and mash
coarsely with a fork,
adding the olive oil
followed by the cumin
and a little salt.

serves 4: 2 large, double loin chops of milk-fed veal, 30 cm x 7 cm   100 ml olive oil
for braising: 1 carrot   1 onion   4 garlic cloves   100 ml groundnut oil   1/2 orange   1/2 lemon
1 bouquet garni   2–3 veal bones   3 tbsp veal stock (page 126)   500 ml white stock (page 126)   salt
pepper   1 tbsp sherry vinegar   **glaze:** 100 g caster sugar   100 ml wine vinegar   juice of 1 orange
juice of 2 lemons   1 tbsp veal stock   zest from the citrus fruit, blanched   1/2 tsp white pepper
wines: Italy: red Piedmont 1996 Barbera d'Asti Pomorosso Coppo
France: Bordeaux red Saint-Julien 1997 Les Fiefs de Lagrange

braised milk-fed veal
meat

1 Trim both pieces of veal and brown them on both sides in the oil in a flameproof casserole. Remove the veal and set aside. **2** Fry the finely diced carrot and onion and the chopped garlic gently in the oil, spreading these out in an even layer; add the orange and lemon halves and the bouquet garni. Put the veal bones on top and return the meat to the casserole, add the veal stock and enough white stock to come half-way up the contents. Season with salt and pepper, cover and cook in a preheated oven at 170°C/gas mark 3 for 3–4 hours. Baste the meat frequently to keep it moist. **3** When the meat is very tender, transfer to another dish and keep warm. **4** Strain the juices though a fine conical sieve; boil to reduce if necessary. Season and add the sherry vinegar. **5** To make the glaze, heat the sugar until melted and caramelized. Remove from the heat, pour in the vinegar and citrus juices and cook, uncovered until reduced by half. Add the veal stock and boil until thickened and syrupy. Add the shredded citrus zests and pepper. **6** Brush liberally over the veal and place in a hot oven to 'set' the glaze. Repeat the glazing and drying process 2 or 3 times.

▼ **accompaniment**

provençal vegetables

2 large aubergines
olive oil
salt
pepper
2 large, ripe tomatoes
1 courgette
1 long, thin aubergine
4 garlic cloves, finely chopped
2 sprigs of marjoram
freshly grated Parmesan

Slice the large aubergines in half lengthwise, scoop out the flesh, brush the 'shells' with a little oil. Season and bake in a preheated oven at 200°C/gas mark 6 for 20 minutes. Peel and deseed the tomatoes and finely dice them, the courgette and the thin aubergine. Sweat with the garlic in 1 tbsp olive oil. Season and stir in the chopped tomatoes. Spoon into the aubergine shells, sprinkle with the marjoram and Parmesan and return to the oven, heated to 220°C/gas mark 7, for 10 minutes.

serves 4: 1/2 tsp cumin seeds   1 tbsp ajowan spice seeds
1/2 tsp cardamom seeds   1/2 tsp nigella seeds   1/2 tsp coriander seeds
320 g muesli   pork bones, crushed   500 ml groundnut oil   80 g butter
100 ml honey   200 ml dry white wine   1 tbsp mustard
scant tsp traditional mustard   40 g chopped gherkins   1/2 tsp sherry vinegar
8 pork medallions weighing 60 g each   2 eggs, beaten
wines: **Argentina:** red Mendoza 1996 Malbec Catena Alta
France: Bordeaux red Saint-Estèphe 1997 Château La Tour de Marbuzet

meat
pork medallions with
spicy muesli coating

1 Roast the cumin, ajowan, cardamom, nigella and coriander seeds in a dry frying pan over a low heat. Grind finely in a coffee grinder, cover and keep dry. **2** Mix the muesli with 1/2 tsp of the freshly ground spices in the food processor. **3** Brown the bones well in a sauté pan in the groundnut oil and butter, then pour off the excess fat and oil. **4** Reduce the heat to very low, add the honey and heat until caramelized. Add the remaining ground spices. **5** Pour in the white wine and simmer until evaporated. Add enough water to dissolve all the deposits and boil again until it has evaporated. Repeat with fresh water three times, then add enough to cover. Simmer until thickened. Strain through a conical sieve, beat in the mustards and stir in the gherkins, followed by the sherry vinegar. Keep hot. **6** Dip the pork medallions into the beaten egg, then coat them evenly in the spicy muesli mixture. Fry until golden brown. **7** Serve the pork medallions with the spicy gravy.

174

sauce ▲ gherkin and onion mustard relish 116   **accompaniment** ▲ straw potatoes 156

serves 4: 4 loins of very young Welsh mountain lamb, weighing 200 g each   salt   pepper
marinade: 1/2 tsp chopped Espelette (mild) chillies   250 ml olive oil   3 garlic cloves
wild thyme flowers   1 bay leaf   **sweet and spicy relish:** 2 finely chopped red onions
large pinch of ground Espelette chillies   55 ml olive oil   salt   60 g garlic cloves
80 g dried apricots   80 g dried dates   50 g pequillos   1 preserved lemon, thinly sliced
50 g currants   25 g capers   3 tbsp concentrated lamb stock
1 tbsp flaked, toasted almonds   1 tbsp roasted pine nuts
wines: United States: red Contra Costa County 1995 Mataro Old Telegram
Bonny Doon **France:** Côtes-du-Rhône red 1997
Châteauneuf du Pape Les Bartavelles Colombo

roast mountain lamb with
sweet and spicy relish

meat

1 To make the marinade, combine the ingredients. **2** Add the lamb to the marinade, turn to coat and leave in a cool place to marinate for 12 hours, turning occasionally. **3** Brown the lamb over a high heat in a large frying pan, then spit-roast or roast in a preheated oven at 250°C/gas mark 9 for 10 minutes. Season and leave to rest. **4** To make the sweet and spicy relish, sweat the onions with the chilli powder in the oil. **5** Add a little salt and cook gently for 20 minutes. Add the thinly sliced garlic and continue cooking for 5–10 minutes. **6** Thinly slice the apricots, dates, pequillos and lemon and stir in along with the currants and capers. **7** Cook gently for 5 minutes, adjust the seasoning and moisten with a little of the loin cooking juices. **8** Add the stock and sprinkle with the almonds and pine nuts.

175

serves 4: 4 farmed pigeons with giblets, weighing 450 g each   500 ml groundnut oil
10 juniper berries   1 large onion   2 garlic cloves   200 ml dry red wine
1.5 litres white stock (page 126)   salt   pepper
wines: United States: red Sonoma County 1996 Pinot noir West Block Rochioli
France: Bordeaux red Saint Julien 1988 Château Léoville Las Cases

poultry barbecued pigeons

1 To prepare the pigeons see step 1, page 156, then cook on a barbecue. Finish the cooking in a hot oven if necessary. **2** Fry the chopped and crushed giblets in the oil in a deep frying pan. Drain off the oil and add the crushed juniper berries, the finely chopped onion and garlic. Fry gently without allowing to brown at all. Stir in the wine and boil until almost completely evaporated. **3** Add 50 ml of white stock and reduce again until almost evaporated. Repeat three more times. **4** Then add enough stock to cover the ingredients in the pan and simmer gently until the sauce is a coating consistency. Strain through a conical sieve. Reheat, season if necessary and serve.

176

sauce ▲ spring relish 110   accompaniment ▲ noodle and asparagus moulds 160

178

Japanese in origin (*bento* means 'cold takeaway meal'), our elegant picnic boxes contain these complete meals interpreted à la française. They are ideal for a 20-minute meal, with time for a glass of wine and a cup of coffee. Anyone who is rushed – or famished – can enjoy bento sitting at the bar, or can take them away to eat elsewhere.

bento

6

desserts

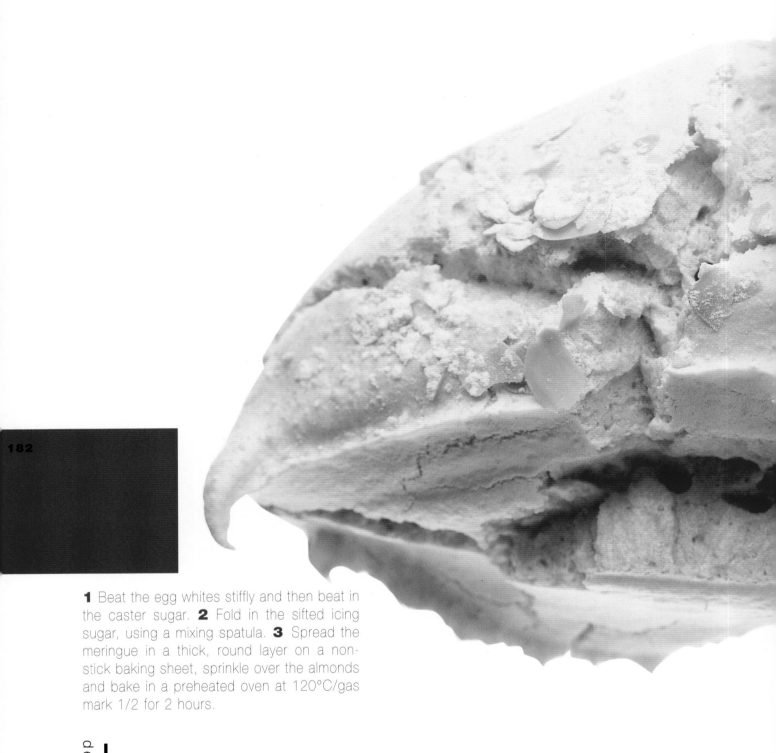

1 Beat the egg whites stiffly and then beat in the caster sugar. **2** Fold in the sifted icing sugar, using a mixing spatula. **3** Spread the meringue in a thick, round layer on a non-stick baking sheet, sprinkle over the almonds and bake in a preheated oven at 120°C/gas mark 1/2 for 2 hours.

desserts

big meringue

serves 4: 250 g (6 large) very fresh egg whites   250 g caster sugar   250 g icing sugar
25 g slivered or flaked almonds

serves 5: 20 sugar bananas (very small sweet bananas)   30 g butter   25 g caster sugar   100 ml rum   2 dried banana slices   2 tbsp icing sugar   **vanilla ice cream:** 500 ml full-cream milk   500 ml whipping cream   seeds from 1 vanilla pod   7 egg yolks   150 g caster sugar
chocolate sauce: 335 g sugar   125 g cocoa powder   125 ml double cream
crème Chantilly: 100 ml crème fraîche   seeds from 1/2 vanilla pod
wines: Austria: white   Neusiedlersee-Hugelland   1995   Pinot blanc   Rusterbeerenauslese   M. Landauer
France: South-west: white   1996   Jurançon   Clos Uroulat   Charles Hours

crunchy bananas
with vanilla ice cream

1 To make the vanilla ice cream, bring the milk and whipping cream very slowly to the boil with the vanilla seeds. Meanwhile, whisk the egg yolks with the caster sugar until pale and thick. Whisk in the hot milk in a thin stream, then pour into the top of a double boiler and stir until the custard is thick enough to coat the back of a spoon. **2** Strain through a fine conical sieve and leave to cool before churning in an ice cream maker. **3** Cook the bananas in the hot butter and sugar, then add the rum. Set aside. **4** Cut the dried bananas lengthwise into strips, dry further in the oven on a buttered baking sheet then dust with icing sugar. **5** To make the chocolate sauce, stir 250 ml water into the sugar and cocoa in a saucepan until smooth then bring to the boil. Stir in the double cream, return to the boil and set aside. **6** To make the crème Chantilly, whisk the crème fraîche with the vanilla seeds until very firm. **7** Arrange 5 cooked bananas in each of 4 rectangular dishes. Top with the crème Chantilly, a rounded tablespoonful of vanilla ice cream and finish with small pieces of dried bananas. Serve with a small jug of the chocolate sauce.

184

serves 6: vegetable oil for deep-frying   **doughnuts:** 450 g strong plain flour
60 g caster sugar, plus extra for coating   15 g instant dried yeast   170 ml full-cream milk
170 g butter, softened   salt   4 eggs   **red fruit compote:** 500 g small strawberries
200 g caster sugar   1 gelatine leaf   100 g redcurrants   50 g mulberries   100 g bilberries
wines: Germany: white Rheingau 1995 Riesling Eiswein Kiedricher Grafenberg Robert Weil
France: Bordeaux white 1995 Loupiac Château du Cros M. Boyer

desserts

spoon's doughnuts
red fruit compote

1 To make the doughnuts, mix the ingredients in the bowl of a food mixer with the dough hook until the dough leaves the sides of the bowl cleanly. Leave to rise for 2 hours at room temperature, then knead briefly. **2** Roll out to 3.5 cm thick and cut out discs using a 10 cm pastry cutter. **3** Use a 3 cm diameter cutter to cut holes from the centre of each one. **4** Transfer to one or more lightly floured baking sheets, well spaced out and leave to rise at room temperature. **5** Half-fill a deep-fryer with oil and heat to 180°C and fry the doughnuts. Transfer to kitchen paper to drain, then roll in caster sugar while still warm. **6** Make the red fruit compote while the dough is rising. Put the strawberries and 1 tbsp sugar in the top of a double boiler over hot water and cover with clingfilm to retain all their scent and flavour. **7** When the strawberries have released all their juice, push them through a conical sieve. Pour the juice back into the double boiler; add the gelatine (soaked in cold water to soften, then drained) and leave to dissolve. **8** Mix in the other fruits and the remaining sugar, then cook over a medium heat for 3–5 minutes. Chill until required, stirring occasionally. **9** Serve the hot doughnuts with the compote.

makes 1 large mille-feuille: 100 g icing sugar   8–10 firm dessert apples   20 g sugar   20 g butter   **caramel parfait:** 200 g sugar   8 large egg yolks   250 ml full-cream milk   75 ml double cream   275 ml crème fraîche, whisked
puff pastry: 280 g plain flour   12 g salt   225 g unsalted butter
wines: Hungary: white   1995   Tokji Aszu   Six Puttonyos   Château Sarospatak
France: Côtes-du-Rhône   white 1995   Hermitage   Vin de paille   J.-L. Grippat

caramelized apple
mille-feuille
caramel parfait

1 Start to make the pastry a day in advance. Mix the flour, the salt and 140 ml water together and shape into a ball. Put in a clean, damp cloth and chill for 2 hours. **2** Meanwhile, press and roll the butter with a rolling pin to soften it. Shape into a large square. **3** Divide the chilled dough in half. Roll into 2 long rectangles and place one on top of the other at right angles, forming a cross. Put the butter in the centre of the cross. Fold one flap of the top dough over it, then fold over the other flap. Fold the flaps of the lower piece of dough over the butter, completely enclosing it in a parcel. Roll the dough lightly, from the centre outwards, into a long, thick rectangle. Fold one-third of the dough over to reach two-thirds of the way along the rectangle, then fold the remaining third over. Turn the pastry through 45° so that the 'fold' is facing you. Roll out lightly again into a rectangle and repeat the folding. Chill for 20 minutes. Repeat the rolling, folding and turning twice more. Wrap in clingfilm and refrigerate overnight. **4** The next morning, roll out the pastry lightly to a 2 mm thick sheet to just fit a large, rectangular baking sheet. **5** Lightly prick the surface with a fork, cover with greaseproof paper and then another baking sheet. **6** Bake in a preheated oven at 180°C/gas mark 4 for 15 minutes. Remove from the oven. Turn up the thermostat to 250°C/gas mark 9. **7** Remove the top baking sheet and the paper and sift icing sugar over the surface. Return to the oven until crisp and pale golden brown. **8** Meanwhile, peel the apples and cut each one into 6, alternatively, use a melon baller. Heat the sugar and butter in a frying pan until caramelized, then add the apples and cook until golden brown. Leave to cool. **9** To make the parfait, use 100 g of the sugar, the eggs and milk to prepare a crème anglaise (step 1, page 184). Heat the remaining sugar until caramelized, and heat the double cream separately until very hot at the same time. Off the heat, stir into the caramel then add to the crème anglaise. **10** Whisk occasionally until cold. Fold in the crème fraîche. Churn in an ice cream maker. **11** Cut the pastry into 3 rectangles. **12** Place some parfait on one pastry sheet, cover with a pastry layer, arrange the apple on top and cover with the remaining pastry. **13** If individual mille-feuilles are preferred, cut the pastry into 15 rectangles at step 5.

190

London

serves 6–8: topping: 850 g full-fat soft cheese   250 g caster sugar   40 g plain flour
4 whole eggs and 2 extra yolks   60 ml double cream
base: 175 g butter   200 g flour   80 g caster sugar   large pinch of salt   3 egg yolks

our favourite
cheesecake

desserts

1 To make the base, make pâte sucrée by mixing 100 g butter, the flour, sugar, salt and beaten egg yolks. Roll into a thin sheet. Transfer to a baking sheet and cook in a preheated oven at 180°C/gas mark 4 for about 20 minutes. **2** Leave to cool, then break into crumbs and work in the remaining butter and chill for 1 hour. **3** Press into the base of a 23 cm diameter springform cake tin. Cover with greaseproof paper and bake in a preheated oven at 180°C/gas mark 4 for about 20 minutes. **4** To make the topping, mix the soft cheese and sugar then fold in the sifted flour. Stir and fold in the eggs one at a time, then add the 2 extra yolks. **5** Stir in the cream to make a smooth and velvety mixture without any lumps. Pour onto the crumble base and bake in a preheated oven at 180°C/gas mark 4 for about 1 1/4 hours. **6** Leave to cool, then chill for 1 hour. Carefully remove from the tin. **7** Serve with a red fruit compote (page 186) or a yogurt sorbet.

serves 4: ice cream: 15 g milk powder   100 ml whipping cream   500 ml full-cream milk   2 egg yolks   175 g caster sugar   35 g unsalted butter   50 g full-fat soft cheese
crumble: 100 g butter   100 g icing sugar   pinch of salt   100 g plain flour   75 g ground almonds   **vanilla sauce:** 250 g single cream   25 g caster sugar   1/2 vanilla pod

cheesecake ice cream sundae

1 To make the ice cream, first whisk the milk powder into the cream. Make a crème anglaise (step 1, page 184) with the milk, whisked cream, egg yolks and sugar. When cooked, add the butter. **2** Cool quickly by placing the top of the double boiler in a bowl of iced water. Chill overnight. **3** To make the crumble, dice the butter, then rub it into the sugar, salt, flour and ground almonds until the mixture resembles fine breadcrumbs. Spread in a baking tray and chill. Bake for 20 minutes in a preheated oven at 170°C/gas mark 3. Leave to cool. **4** To make the vanilla sauce, pour the cream into a saucepan, add the sugar and the vanilla pod (cut open along its length on one side) and simmer, uncovered, until reduced by one-third. Remove from the heat, discard the vanilla and leave to cool in a bowl. **5** To assemble the dessert, churn the ice cream mixture with the cream cheese in an ice cream maker until firmly frozen. Spoon some red fruit compote (page 186) into each dish, or use a selection of fresh summer berries. Top each with a scoop of ice cream, pour over vanilla sauce, and finish with the crumble mixture.

serves 4: herb and spice infusion: 100 g sugar   1 small bunch of peppermint sprigs   1 small bunch of spearmint   1/2 lemon grass bulb   1/2 hyssop leaf   2 star anise   10 g white peppercorns, coarsely crushed   1/2 vanilla pod   2 cardamom pods   zest of 1 orange and 1 lemon   **guava and passion fruit sorbet:** 160 g caster sugar   60 g glucose syrup   500 g passion fruits   250 g guava flesh, seeds removed   **fruit salad:** 1/2 ripe Indian mango   1 kiwi fruit   1/2 ripe papaya   1/2 small pineapple   100 g lychees   100 g puréed apricots

wines: South Africa: white   Le Cap   1998   Sauvignon noble   Late Harvest   Klein Constancia   **France:** Côtes-du-Rhône   white   1996   Condrieu Les Éguets   Cuilleron

tropical fruit salad with puréed apricots guava and passion fruit sorbet herb and spice infusion

desserts

1 To make the herb and spice infusion, heat 500 ml water with the sugar, stirring, until the sugar dissolves, then bring to the boil. Remove from the heat and add the herbs, spices and zest. Cover with a tight fitting lid and leave for 24 hours. **2** To make the sorbet, heat 250 ml water with the sugar and glucose until the sugar has dissolved then boil to make a syrup. Cool quickly. **3** Cut the passion fruits in half, scoop out the contents and mix briefly with a hand-held whisk. Strain through a conical sieve and mix the liquid with the guavas and the cooled sugar syrup. Transfer to an ice cream maker and churn until firm. **4** To make the salad, finely dice the fruit and stir into the apricot purée. **5** Spoon a layer of fruit salad into 4 deep plates and top with a rounded tablespoonful of sorbet. Serve the herb and spice infusion separately.

193

serves 4: **margarita sorbet:** 200 g caster sugar   110 g glucose syrup   15 g milk powder
2 tbsp tequila   250 ml lime juice   **lime jelly:** 200 g caster sugar   2 limes   1 lemon
2 gelatine leaves   **topping:** 2 Florida pink grapefruit   3 Moroccan oranges
wines: United States: white Napa Valley 1995 Sauvignon-Sémillon Dolce Far Niente
France: Champagne Paul Drouet Special Reserve Selected by Alain Ducasse

desserts

citrus fruits in
fresh lime jelly
margarita sorbet

194

Tokyo

1 To make the margarita sorbet, bring 450 ml water, the sugar and glucose to the boil to make a syrup. **2** Remove from the heat and stir in the milk powder, tequila and lime juice. Leave to cool. Churn in an ice cream maker **3** To make the jelly, heat the sugar in 200 ml water, stirring until the sugar dissolves then boil to 30°C. Measure 250 ml and leave for 30 minutes to infuse over the lowest possible heat with the limes and lemon. **4** Cool slightly and remove the fruit before adding the gelatine leaves (soaked in cold water to soften, then drained). When completely dissolved, leave in a cool place. **5** Cut off all the peel and pith from the grapefruits and oranges and remove the segments from the thin inner skin. Cut each segment lengthwise into 2 or 3 very thin slices. **6** Arrange in an overlapping layer on each plate and cover with a thin layer of the lime jelly. **7** Chill until required, then add a rounded tablespoonful of the margarita sorbet.

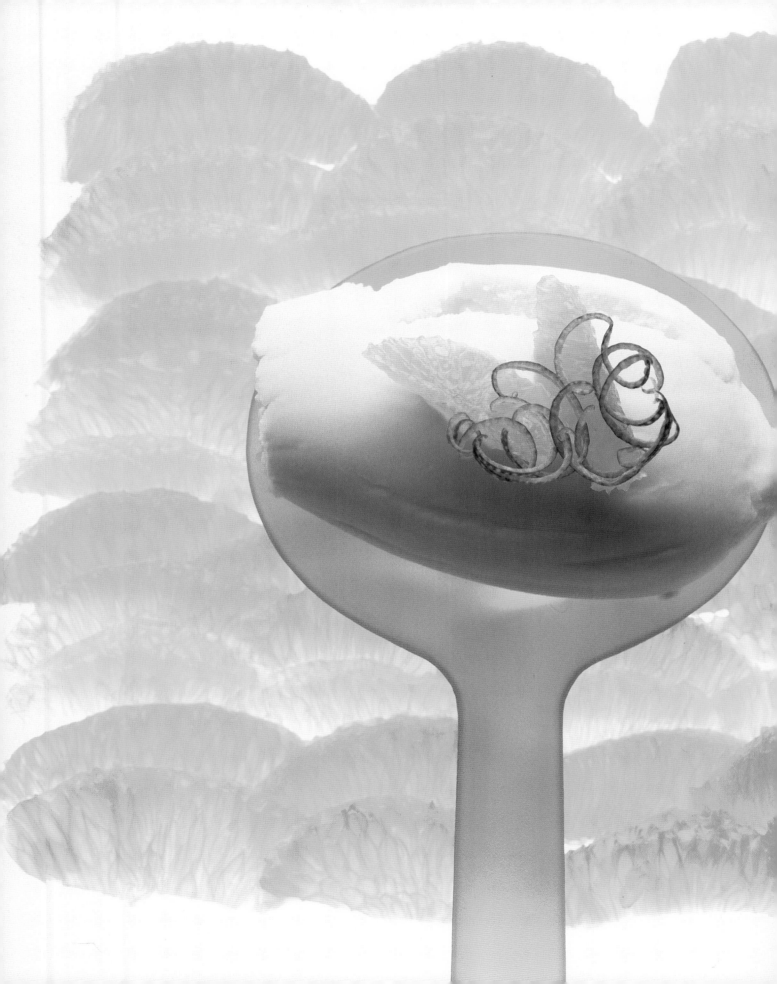

Spoon's chocolate pizza

1 Make the brioche dough a day ahead. Mix the yeast with the lukewarm water in the bowl of a food mixer. Add the flour, salt, sugar and cocoa powder and mix to a fairly firm dough at medium speed setting. Gradually add the lightly beaten eggs, a little at a time. **2** Stop adding the beaten eggs when the dough is smooth and leaves the sides of the bowl cleanly. Now add the butter and stop mixing when the dough leaves the sides of the bowl cleanly again. Cover with a damp cloth and leave at warm room temperature until risen. Knead briefly and shape into a ball. Put in a large, lightly-floured bowl, cover with a cloth and leave at room temperature overnight. **3** Roll out to 1 cm thick. Cut out 6 discs, each 12 cm in diameter and put them in greased non-stick tart tins. Prick lightly with a fork and sprinkle over the cocoa powder and sugar for the topping, using a teaspoon. Dot with small flakes of butter. **4** Leave to rise. **5** Bake in a preheated oven at 190°C/gas mark 5 until three-quarters done and then drizzle the cream over the surface. **6** Return to the oven. As soon as the topping looks syrupy, add the chopped chocolate and bake for about 2 minutes until melted. **7** Serve warm.

makes 6 pizzas: **brioche dough:** 10 g instant dried yeast   1 tbsp lukewarm water
250 g strong plain flour   8 g salt   20 g caster sugar   12 g cocoa powder
3 eggs   175 g butter   **chocolate topping:** 20 g cocoa powder
35 g molasses sugar or muscovado sugar   25 g butter   50 ml single cream
50 g plain chocolate with at least 70% cocoa solids, chopped
wines: South Africa: red Paarl 1979 Cinsault-Tinto-Barocca
Souzao Cavendish KWV
France: Roussillon red 1993 Maury Mas Amiel

serves 6: 6 reinettes or Cox's apples   25 g caster sugar   15 g butter
pains perdu: 200 g sugar   1 litre full-cream milk   4 eggs   pinch of salt
6 slices slightly stale white country bread   25 g butter

pain perdu
caramelized apple squares

1 Core the apples and make shallow cuts in their skin as usual for baked apples to prevent the skins bursting. Place in a buttered ovenproof dish, sprinkle with the caster sugar and dot with flakes of butter. Bake in a preheated oven at 180°C/gas mark 4, basting occasionally, until very tender but not 'collapsed'. **2** Remove from the oven and immediately shape the apples into squares, pressing against their sides and tops with one or more spatulas. **3** To make the pains perdu, stir 100 g of the sugar into the milk in a bowl. Beat the eggs with the salt. Dip the bread in the milk, then in the eggs. **4** Heat the butter and the remaining sugar in a frying pan until caramelized. **5** Add the bread and fry until golden brown. **6** Place an apple on each plate, top with pain perdu and place a scoop of vanilla ice cream on top (page 184).

1 To make the ice cream, mix the milk, egg yolks and 80 g of the sugar in a heatproof bowl. **2** Cook the remaining sugar over a moderate heat in a small, heavy saucepan until it melts and caramelizes. At the same time; bring the cream to the boil and pour onto the caramel. **3** Pour into the heatproof bowl, place over a double boiler base and cook, stirring, until the custard coats the back of the spoon. Immediately place the bowl in iced water. **4** To make the fudge, heat both types of sugar, the glucose syrup and milk in a saucepan to 125°C. Remove from the heat and stir in the vanilla pod, salt and butter. Pour into a square mould and leave to set. **5** Churn the caramel ice cream mixture in an ice cream maker, adding the fudge, cut into very small squares, near the end of the process. **6** To make the caramel sauce, heat the caster sugar in a small, heavy saucepan until it caramelizes. At the same time, bring the cream to the boil, then pour into the caramel. **7** Place 3 scoops of caramel ice cream in each dish and pour over caramel sauce.

caramel ice cream
with caramel sauce

serves 4: caramel ice cream: 500 ml milk   4 egg yolks   260 g caster sugar   150 ml single cream
fudge: 300 g unrefined cane sugar   30 g caster sugar   60 g glucose syrup   300 ml milk
1/2 vanilla pod   pinch of salt   60 g butter   **caramel sauce:** 150 g caster sugar   200 g single cream

makes 100 biscuits: black biscuits: 340 g butter   725g unrefined cane sugar
675 g plain flour   15 g salt   4 eggs   365 g walnuts
720 g plain chocolate with at least 70% cocoa solids, finely grated
white biscuits: 340 g butter   540 g sugar   3 whole eggs   520 g plain flour   10 g salt
270 g pecan nuts   400 g good quality white chocolate

black biscuits
white biscuits

desserts

1 To make the black biscuits, beat the butter with the sugar in a food processor until pale and creamy. Add the sifted flour and salt, and the lightly beaten eggs. **2** Fold in the walnuts and the chocolate. Leave to stand for 1 hour in a cool place or in the refrigerator. **3** Break off small pieces about 1 cm long, shape into balls between your palms and flatten slightly. Place on a baking sheet. **4** Bake in a preheated oven at 200°C/gas mark 6 for up to 5 minutes; they should be soft and slightly chewy. **5** Quickly transfer to a cooling rack. **6** Make the white cookies in the same way.

199

1 A day in advance, bring the milk to the boil, remove from the heat and immediately add the Malabar. Leave overnight at room temperature. **2** The next day, transfer to the upper part of a double boiler, stir in the remaining ingredients and heat, stirring, until the custard coats the back of the spoon. **3** Strain through a conical sieve into a bowl to get rid of any undissolved gum. Place the bowl in iced water. When cold, refrigerate to allow the flavour to develop. **4** Churn in an ice cream maker.

desserts

malabar ice cream

serves 10: zest of 1 lemon   zest of 1 lime   **sweet pastry:** 150 g butter   95 g icing sugar   250 g plain flour   1 egg   30 g ground almonds   salt   seeds from 1/2 vanilla pod   **lemon cream:** 550 g lump sugar   unwaxed lemons, to yield 400 ml juice (see step 2)   10 eggs   750 g unsalted butter   1 gelatine leaf   **lemon sauce:** 75 g icing sugar   100 ml lemon juice   2 eggs   50 g butter, melted   **wines: United States:** white   Santa Cruz Mountains   1996   Muscat Canelli   Vin de glacière/Ice cream maker's wine   Bonny Doon   **France:** Alsace   white   1996   Riesling   Vin de glace/Ice cream wine   J.-P. Bechtold

lemon cream tarts

desserts

1 To make the pastry, mix the butter with the sifted icing sugar, adding the sifted flour, the lightly beaten egg, ground almonds, a large pinch of salt and the vanilla seeds. Wrap in clingfilm and chill overnight. **2** To make the lemon cream, rub all the surfaces of the sugar cubes against the lemons' skins before squeezing them. Put the sugar cubes in the upper compartment of a double boiler, squeeze the required amount of lemon juice and add to the cubes. Stir in the lightly beaten eggs. **3** Cook, stirring, until the mixture coats the back of the spoon. Remove from the heat and to cool to 50°C. Stir in the butter, a small piece at a time, followed immediately by the gelatine (pre-soaked to soften, then drained). When dissolved set aside in a cool place or the fridge. **4** To make the lemon sauce, combine the sugar and lemon juice then add the lightly beaten eggs. Stir in the butter. **5** Roll out the pastry very thinly and use to line 10 deep tartlet tins 10 cm in diameter, and 10 tartlet tins 6 cm in diameter. **6** Bake blind in a preheated oven at 150°C/gas mark 2 for 20–25 minutes. Leave to cool slightly then carefully transfer to a wire rack. **7** Put the smaller cases on a baking sheet and fill with lemon cream. Return to the oven, close the door and immediately turn off the oven. **8** When the lemon custard has set, transfer to a rack to cool. **9** Place these tarts in the centre of the larger pastry cases and fill the empty 'moat' with lemon sauce, using a pastry bag and nozzle. **10** Decorate with very fine strips of blanched lemon and lime zest.

Mauritius

serves 12: coconut ice cream (page 206)   **crumble:** 500 g butter   500 g caster sugar   500 g plain flour   375 g ground almonds   **pineapple layer:** 250 g pineapple flesh   75 g caster sugar   3 gelatine leaves   **rum sultanas:** 50 g sultanas soaked in 3 tbsp golden rum
wines: Hungary: white 1995 Tokaji Aszu Six Puttonyos Château Sarospatak
France: Bordeaux white 1994 Sauternes Cru Barrejats

desserts

iced pineapple and coconut ice cream sandwich with a
crumble base

1 Make the crumble a day in advance (step 3, page 192) and leave to dry, uncovered, at room temperature overnight. **2** Also start preparing the pineapple layer a day in advance. Process the pineapple to a smooth pulp and boil in a non-stick saucepan with the sugar over a high heat, stirring until the liquid has evaporated. Remove from the heat and add the gelatine (pre-soaked in water, then drained). **3** When dissolved, stir and pour into a 20 cm cake tin with a removable base. Freeze overnight. **4** The next day, remove the frozen pineapple from the tin and return to the freezer. **5** Cover the base of the cake tin with the crumble, pressing it down well. Bake in a preheated oven at 170°C/gas mark 3 for 15 minutes. Leave to cool then put on a serving plate and sprinkle with the drained sultanas. Put the frozen pineapple carefully on top and cover with scoops of coconut ice cream. Return to the freezer for 2 hours before serving.

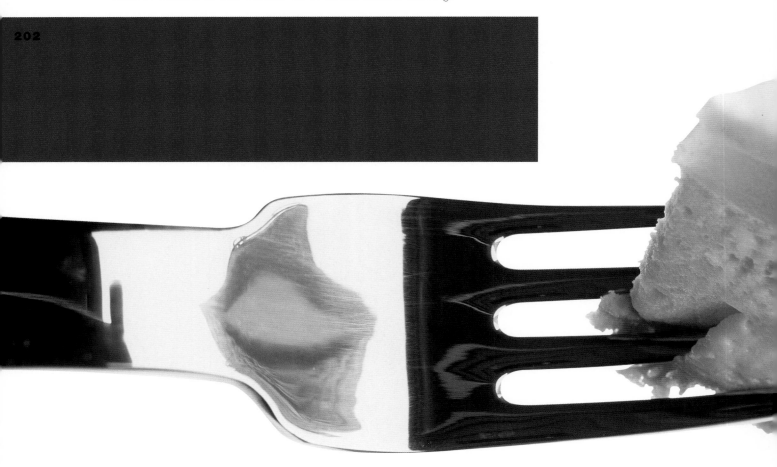

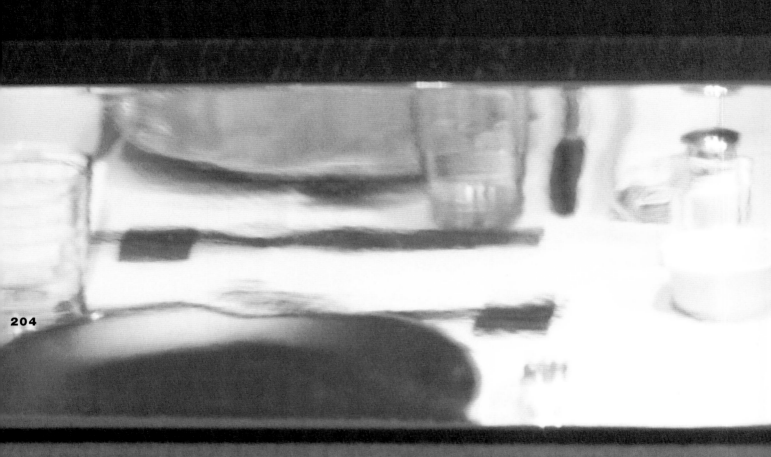

1 To make the peppermint sorbet, soak the fresh mint in 355 ml water and the mint essence for several hours. Remove the fresh mint. Mix the sugar, glucose syrup and milk powder together and add to the mint-flavoured water. **2** Churn the sorbet mixture in an ice cream maker. **3** To make the chocolate pastry, combine the well-creamed butter with the flour and salt, using your fingertips. Add the baking powder and cocoa, sifting these in together while stirring. **4** Beat the egg yolks with the sugar until very pale and fluffy; add to the chocolate mixture, working them only just enough to combine evenly. Chill in the fridge for 1–2 hours. **5** Roll out the pastry and cut into twelve 7 x 8 cm rectangles. Place on a baking sheet and bake in a preheated oven at 170°C/gas mark 3 for about 15 minutes. Transfer to a wire rack to cool. **6** Put a well-rounded tablespoonful of sorbet on each pastry base. Decorate with sprigs of mint **7** Serve with chocolate sauce (page 184) and crème Chantilly (page 184).

desserts

after spoon

serves 12: peppermint sorbet: 1 bunch of fresh peppermint
1–2 drops natural peppermint essence   105 g sugar   30 g glucose syrup   10 g milk powder
chocolate pastry: 250 g butter   500 g plain flour   5 g salt   20 g baking powder
25 g cocoa powder   5 egg yolks   200 g caster sugar   sprigs of mint, to decorate

1 To make the ice cream, stir the ingredients together in a double boiler until the temperature reaches 85° C. Cool quickly by placing in a bowl of cold water and ice. When cold, chill for 1–2 hours to allow the flavour to develop. Churn in an ice cream maker until thick. **2** Transfer to a freezer until hardened but still soft enough to scoop into balls with an ice cream scoop. Push a lolly stick securely into each scoop. **3** Roll each ice cream lolly in some sifted cocoa powder to coat, then return to the freezer. **4** To make the caramel sauce, see step 6, page 198. **5** Place 3 lollies on each plate and serve the caramel sauce separately.

milk chocolate and caramel ice lollies

desserts

serves 4: chocolate ice cream: 500 ml full-cream milk   100 ml single cream   50 g milk powder
5 egg yolks   175 g fresh coconut flesh   35 g glucose syrup   125 g caster sugar
caramel sauce: 200 ml single cream   150 g caster sugar   **coating:**   240 g cocoa powder

serves 12: 200 g couverture chocolate, melted   25 g cocoa powder
coconut meringue: 150 g finely grated fresh coconut   75 g icing sugar, sifted   25 g plain flour
4 very fresh egg whites   75 g caster sugar   **white chocolate mousse:** 200 ml coconut milk
600 g good quality white chocolate   100 ml Malibu   1 litre double cream
chocolate sauce: 120 g cocoa powder   1 litre milk   120 g caster sugar
wines: South Africa: red Paarl 1979 Cinsault-Tinta Barocca Souzao Cavendish KWV
France: Rousillon red 1993 Banyuls La Coume Domaine du Mas Blanc Docteur Parce

chocolate fingers
iced white chocolate mousse and meringues

1 To make the meringue, mix the coconut, icing sugar and flour. Whisk the egg whites until stiff, then gradually whisk in the sugar. Add to the coconut mixture and fold it in. Spread out fairly thinly in two 25 x 15 x 2.5 cm cake frames set on 2 baking sheets and sift over a little extra icing sugar. Bake for 10 minutes in a preheated oven at 180°C/gas mark 4 with the door ajar, until dry. Leave to cool then cut into 12 rectangles. **2** Cover both sides of the meringues in melted chocolate and place in the cake frames. Leave to set. **3** To make the mousse, boil the coconut milk and stir into the finely chopped chocolate until melted. Leave to cool. Stir in the Malibu then fold in the cream, whisked only to very soft peaks. Pour into the cake frames to reach the top. Freeze overnight. Cut into 12 rectangles and return to the freezer. **4** Spread melted couveture chocolate over a sheet of clingfilm to make two 25 x 15 cm chocolate sheets. Leave to set but not harden completely before cutting into 24 rectangles. Carefully cover with another sheet of clingfilm, put between 2 chopping boards and chill. **5** To make the chocolate sauce, cream the sifted cocoa with the milk and sugar and heat in a double boiler. **6** Pipe a wide ring of melted chocolate on a plate and dust the plate with a little sifted cocoa powder. Put 2 meringue and mousse rectangles on each plate with a rectangle of chocolate neatly on top. Serve the chocolate sauce separately.

206

serves 12: brioche: 20 g instant dried yeast   2 tbsp lukewarm water   500 g plain flour   10 g salt   8 eggs   400 g butter   flaked almonds, for sprinkling   3 tbsp icing sugar, to decorate
almond milk ice cream: 1 egg yolk   10 g glucose syrup   210 ml milk   12 g milk powder   50 g whipping cream   25 g good quality almond paste   25 ml almond milk, preferably Fabbri
nougatine: 75 g caster sugar   25 g lavender honey   75 g butter   75 g chopped almonds
glaze: 1 egg yolk beaten with 1 tbsp milk
wines: South Africa: white Paarl 1979 Chenin blanc Jerepigo KWV

venetian almond
ice cream and
brioche slices

1 Make the brioche dough a day in advance (steps 1–3, page 196). Leave to rise for 1 hour. Knock down and refrigerate overnight. **2** To make the ice cream, make a crème anglais with the egg yolk, glucose syrup, milk with the milk powder whisked in, and the cream (step 1, page 184). Cool slightly then whisk in the chopped almond paste and the almond milk. Cool, then chill. **3** To make the nougatine, cook the sugar and honey until boiling, then add the butter and almonds. Pour quickly into a large baking tray and bake in a preheated oven at 170°C/gas mark 3 for about 25 minutes. Leave to cool. Chop coarsely. **4** Roll the brioche dough to 3 cm thick and cut into twelve 5 x 8 cm rectangles. Brush with the glaze and sprinkle with the nougatine. **5** Leave to prove for 30 minutes before placing on a baking tray in a preheated oven at 190°C/gas mark 5 for about 15 minutes. Cool on a wire rack, then cut in half lengthwise **6** Churn the ice cream mixture in an ice cream maker until almost firm. Spoon into a piping bag fitted with a wide plain nozzle. **7** Pipe the ice cream onto half the brioche rectangles, sprinkle with almonds and place another rectangle on top. Dust with sifted icing sugar.

Note: The slices can also be made with three layers each.

SIECLE

serves 4: **vanilla syrup:** 300 g sugar   seeds from 1 vanilla pod
strawberry syrup: 1 kg small, ripe strawberries   400 g sugar
granita of citrus fruits: 100 ml orange juice   100 ml lime juice   100 ml lemon juice
100 ml Florida pink grapefruit juice   200 ml Perrier water   150 g sugar
selection of red fruits, such as: strawberries, raspberries, mulberries, wild strawberries
wines: Australia: white McLaren Vale 1996 Riesling Noble D'Arenberg
France: Loire Valley white Anjou 1998 Côteaux du Layon Grains nobles Patrick Baudoin

desserts

the ultimate red fruit salad
citrus granita

1 To make the vanilla syrup, heat 1 litre water with the sugar and vanilla, stirring to dissolve the sugar, then bring to the boil. Remove from the heat and leave to infuse. **2** To make the strawberry syrup, mix the sugar and strawberries in the top of a double boiler and cook very slowly for 4 hours. Drain through a conical sieve without pressing the fruit. Reserve the liquid. **3** To make the granita, mix the fruit juices and Perrier with the sugar, and freeze until firm. **4** Pour a little vanilla syrup into tall glasses and add some strawberry syrup; do not stir as the marbled effect is decorative. Add a portion of the fruits. Lastly, run a fork along the surface of the granita and top the desserts with thin shards of granita.

for 1 large dessert: 8–10 reinette or Cox's apples
200 g caster sugar or unrefined cane sugar
wines: France: Bordeaux 1997 Sydre Argelette Cuvée Prestige Éric Bordelet

apples baked in a
clay brick

desserts

1 Peel the apples, cut them in half and then slice very thinly. Arrange in neat layers in a pre-soaked clay brick (such as a chicken brick), sprinkling each layer with sugar until the brick is three-quarters full. **2** Put on the lid and place in a cold oven. Switch on the oven and set the temperature at 180°C/gas mark 4 and cook for 3 hours. **3** Check on the apples occasionally, turning the brick when necessary to ensure even cooking. **4** Take the clay brick from the oven and leave to cool, just as it is, on a rack until completely cold. **5** Serve the baked apples from the brick and add a scoop of vanilla ice cream (page 184).

211

Spoon food & wine
14, rue de Marignan
75008 Paris
tel.+33 (0)1 40 76 34 44
fax. +33 (0)1 40 76 34 37
e-mail : info@spoon.tm.fr
http://www.spoon.tm.fr
Chef de cuisine: Christophe Moret
Directeur de salle: Christian Laval

Spoon Food and Wine
by Alain Ducasse
1–4 Urayasushi Maihama Chiba
Japon IKSPIARI 317
tel. +81 47 305 5633
fax. +81 47 305 2473
Chef de cuisine: David Bellin
Directeur de salle: Éric Van Hecke

Spoon des îles
by Alain Ducasse
Le Saint-Géran
Poste de Flacq-Île Maurice
tel. +230 401 1551
fax. +230 401 1552
e-mail : spoonrst@sunresort.com
www.spoondesîles.com
Chef de cuisine: Massimo Luvara
Directeur de salle: Denis Novaria
Chef Patissier: Christian Gonthier

Spoon + at Sanderson
50 Berners Street
London W1T 3NG
tel. +44 (0)20 7300 1444
fax. +44 (0)20 7300 1479
e-mail:spoon+@sanderson.
schragerhotels.com
Chef de cuisine: Laurent André
Directeur de salle: Stéphane Davaine

acknowledgements

Alain Ducasse is particularly grateful to Christophe Moret for making this book, with all its recipes, possible.

He also wishes to express his heartfelt gratitude to the entire team of Spoon Food & Wine, Paris, for their patience while the photographs were being taken.

Many thanks to:

Frédéric Vardon for his technical assistance and for looking after the Spoon restaurants' interests worldwide;

Frédéric Rober, Didier Elena and Aude Coronel for their invaluable help in editing the recipes;

Gérard Margeon for his advice on the wines;

Massimo Luvara, Laurent André, David Bellin, Kei Kojima and Christian Gonthier for taking part in the Spoon adventure; all the Spoon teams: at Spoon des Iles, Mauritius at the Saint-Géran resort, Spoon + at Sanderson in London, and Spoon Food & Wine by Alain Ducasse in Tokyo.

A big thank you as well to all those mentioned in this book, without whom Spoon would simply not be what it is.

Harmut Kiefer would like to thank his assistant photographers Sabine Scheckel, New York, Olaf Hirschberg, Cologne and Birgit Œllingrath, Paris.

t   h   e   i

n d e x

Our thanks also go to Karine Bigler,
make up; Ana Donato, hairdressing;
and to Cartier, Nina Gill, Georg Jensen,
Vis-à-Vis, Siècle, CFOC and, of course,
to Sophie for her toy boat.

See you spoon...